Live in Freedom

Reflections on Limits, Dreams and the Essential

Live in Freedom

Reflections on Limits, Dreams and the Essential

Miriam Subirana

BOOKS

Winchester, UK
Washington, USA

First published by O-Books, 2009
Reprinted 2010
O-Books is an imprint of John Hunt Publishing Ltd., Laurel House, Station Approach,
Alresford, Hants, SO24 9JH, UK
office1@o-books.net
www.o-books.com

For distributor details and how to order please visit the 'Ordering' section on our website.

Text copyright: Miriam Subirana 2008

ISBN: 978 1 84694 196 2

A CIP catalogue record for this book is available from the British Library.

Original title: Vivir en Libertad. Reflexiones sobre los límites, los sueños y lo esencial.

Translation: Caroline Wilson

Cover painting: Live your dream I
by Miriam Subirana

Design: Stuart Davies

Printed in the UK by CPI Antony Rowe
Printed in the USA by Offset Paperback Mfrs, Inc

We operate a distinctive and ethical publishing philosophy in all
areas of our business, from our global network of authors to
production and worldwide distribution.

CONTENTS

Prologue   1

Introduction   3

Who Rules in Your Life?   6

The Power of Circumstances   48

Your Inner World: Personal Power   65

Meditation: The Path Towards Freedom of Spirit   90

Being the Creator of Your Destiny   97

Transcend   140

Meditations   145

Bibliography   156

Raja Yoga Meditation Centres of the Brahma Kumaris
      World Spiritual University   159

About the Author   160

I dedicate this book to my friend,
To my soul friend
To the violinist who, playing his strings, awakens the melody in
my heart
To the creative being who, with his energy, makes mine dance
To the friend who is a source of inspiration for painting art
works full of colour,
writing beautiful poems and realising great dreams.
To the friend that loves me
And in his love awakens my beauty
To the friend who accepts me
And thus my defences fall
To the friend who makes me naked
And makes me see the truth without masks
To the free friend
Who in his freedom
Helps me to live out my dreams
And I discover, marvel at myself and enjoy
Each moment of existence

To the eternal friend, who is always
In the light of his being.

Prologue

The reader has in their hands a book on freedom; an occasion to go deep into the core of that which is human; a book that breaks with clichés and stereotypes about freedom. They are before an essay that has the clear will to tune into the person of flesh and bone, with their secret flutterings and their states of wants. A brave book, which goes down into the deepest layers of the human being in order to speak from there a liberating, edifying word, that stimulates us into living a life that is authentically human, worthy of being lived

Beyond the well-worn clichés about what freedom is, the author, Miriam Subirana, opens up to us another mental perspective and links the idea of freedom with that of liberation. Against the fallacious idea that freedom is the arbitrary expression of an ego that primarily satisfies its needs and desires, the writer shows us that freedom is a long journey; difficult, arduous, but possible; a path of liberation, of detachment from all that dominates human beings and keeps them imprisoned in a state of mental, emotional and spiritual alienation. A book written with the heart, but put together with solid arguments, nourished by Western and Eastern sources, with a clear desire to be intelligible for all readers.

Freeing oneself from the voices of the past, from the wounds that history has left stamped on the skin of the soul; freeing oneself of social ties and conventions, from the servitude of the politically correct and the accursed ego that is the main source of slavery: here lies the meaning of this book that, what is more, brings with it guidelines and practical strategies in order to achieve such an end.

Beyond fatalism and social determinism, Miriam Subirana tries out a song to freedom, but without succumbing to ingenuousness. She knows that the task is arduous, but not impossible. She knows that in such an effort freedom is at stake. She knows that this yearning is rooted in the most intimate part of each human being, because she herself, as a person, has lived and experienced it in her inner self.

A book that makes us think. More than a book; it is an invitation to go into oneself, to become aware of what we are, but above all, of what we can become.

Francesc Torralba Roselló

Introduction

Freedom has, throughout history, been one of the values that human beings have most laboured to defend. It has brought about revolutions and rebellions against oppression and injustice. We have achieved great advances in gaining a greater freedom of expression and of beliefs. However, the experience of violence and pain has increased. We haven't known how to use freedom to strengthen ourselves spiritually, emotionally and mentally in order to attain personal balance and harmony in relationships.

We have created habits that influence us, condition us and tie us down; habits that deprive us of our personal freedom. It may even be that such habits come to generate an enslaving or addiction on an emotional and mental level. Freedom is being capable of thinking, experiencing and expressing our thoughts and feelings, without being conditioned by external factors or the negative tendencies of our personality, and without causing pain.

Our creative capacity to choose what we think and what we feel at each moment and how we respond in each situation is our strength and our freedom. However, our beliefs limit us, our past conditions us, and our fears prevent us from living out our deepest dreams.

If we want to live in freedom we have to know ourselves better, question our beliefs, clean out the store cupboard of our memories that keep us anchored in the past, and overcome our fears, which put a brake on us and block our immense creative energy.

In the same way that education is fundamental in order to give the key to the illiterate and the poor and open the doors to their own freedom, educating our spirit is fundamental in order to come out of the ignorance in which we live and thus achieve our full freedom.

To live in freedom means learning to ask ourselves the right questions. This will help us to widen our vision and to be more aware. It is important to ask oneself the right questions in order to be able to receive the answers. Even if we have the answer right in front of us, if we haven't asked the question we will neither receive nor understand the answer. If we can formulate the question, we will see that the answer is already at the threshold of our door.

We live on the basis of a group of beliefs that make up our vision in the face of life, our attitudes, our decisions and our behaviour:

Beliefs that are sociological, psychological, cultural, political, religious and/or spiritual. Beliefs about what is good and what is bad; about what is success and what is failure. And thus an endless amount of beliefs that make up 'our box', in which we live.

Can beliefs free us? Or ultimately, do we have to transcend beliefs? In mystical experience, in contemplative silence, we transcend everything, including our individual self. We enter into the dimension of light.

However, while we are here in this earthly world, let us live well. We have been born to live, not to learn to live. But perhaps we have become rusty, tired or disillusioned because we have forgotten the rules of the game and life has turned into a constant battle and into an obstacle course.

In this book I present you with different ideas, questions and reflections, so that you might embrace life, embrace change and uncertainty. To live is to have pleasure, laugh, accept, deal with, love, and share. Let go of the baggage that you do not need.

When you begin the pilgrimage of the path of Santiago de Compostela, you take many things 'just in case'. After a few kilometres of walking you realise how much unnecessary weight you are carrying and you let it go. You begin to trust that every-thing you need will come to meet you on the path. And you realise that you already have what is most important: life, hope and the energy with which to walk.

On this pilgrimage the destination of freedom is neither far nor outside. It is a second away and a millimetre in distance. It is you and it is in you.

Who Rules in Your Life?

To live in freedom is to direct your own life; to have in your hands the reins of your life and to know how to manage them. What you do is directed towards achieving your aims. You do not live at the mercy of others. You choose at each stage according to what you set out for yourself. You have the clarity of what you want and of the decisions that you take.

To live in freedom you need the power of concentration in order not to become distracted or dispersed, and the power of determination in order to put into practice what you truly long for. You need to respect yourself and to have respect for others and for your surroundings. Since we do not live in isolation, the art of ruling in our own lives requires the skill of synchronising, empathising, listening and dialoguing.

However, the truth is that often we feel trapped, sometimes by destiny or circumstances, other times by people or by money, or health, or by… so many things that surround us and that in some way are extensions of our life. At work we feel pressured by time, by tasks, by colleagues. In the family we feel misunderstood or extremely responsible and worried. Sometimes we feel that we have to submit ourselves to the desires of others in order to please them. Our body does not always collaborate with us; it gets ill, it gets tired, it bothers us and we do not sleep in peace. On a social level, it seems that the consumer society 'gobbles us up' in a race to try to get more, have more, and stand out more. On a personal level, one would like to do something, but it seems that circumstances prevent it; they do not help, they do not support us in achieving it. All this leads us to feel inwardly without freedom.

So we ask ourselves: is it possible to achieve this true freedom of being? Where can we find it? We have to be awake in order to know it and to find it.

Although you believe that this morning you woke up, it is very possible that you are still deeply asleep. Not the kind of sleep that kept you unconscious during the night, but rather the kind of sleep that, on a greater or lesser level, has invaded us all during the day and in our lives. It is the sleep of ignorance. It is the sleep of which you think you are conscious and that you think you are awake, and yet you do not know that you are deceiving yourself. It is the sleep whose power is dormant, that is not aware of what it is thinking nor of the consequences of what it is doing.

You are asleep if you blame others or situations for your feelings of anxiety, stress, worry or fear. All of these feelings are created by you, independently of what the circumstances are. Every time that you blame others for what you feel, you are asleep to reality and to the truth that your feelings are your creation, as a response to the stimuli you receive.

When we are awake we accept full responsibility for our thoughts, our emotions, attitudes, actions, everywhere and always. We should achieve the knowledge of ourselves that will help us to respond consciously and 'awake' in the face of circumstances, situations and people. That way we will experience that feeling of freedom whereby we rule in our life, without allowing external circumstances to dictate our attitudes or pollute our thinking and our feeling without us realising.

True freedom lies in the capacity and the power of choice that we have. We often forget it. And the first choice is: what and how you think. Each thought that goes through your mind is created by you.

We have the freedom to create the thought that we wish to create. Nobody forces us to think in one way or another; nobody can get into our mind, except ourselves. We forget about that freedom and we think on automatic pilot. We let our mind think without even realising what we are thinking. In this way, when there is an external stimulus, whether it is a situation or someone's words, we react automatically without being fully aware of the capacity of choice that we have or of the consequences of our reaction.

With our thoughts, we trap ourselves into negative reactions. We create useless thoughts that take energy away from us. We enter into a spiral of thoughts that create suffering, and more than that, they increase it. For example, we listen to words that hurt us and that we don't like at all. The mind repeats those words, and each time that it repeats them, it recreates the situation that has already happened, increasing the pain and unhappiness. Why did they say this to me? How did they dare to talk to me like that? Why did they say that to me at that moment? Creating these thoughts, we cause our own unhappiness.

With the mind, we repeat and relive situations that have taken place in the past. We don't live the present with the freedom that we could live it with. We trap ourselves with our own thoughts about what has happened, because we don't exercise the power of choosing what we really want to think. We allow a situation, a person, or something, to influence us or have an impact on us – an image, some words, a scene – and we repeat that impact with our thoughts, without realising that we are not using our capacity to choose well; we are choosing to repeat, in our mind, what causes us suffering and traps us into it.

As we become aware of the capacity that we have to control our thoughts, we start to understand that we can choose how we think and how we feel with respect to the circumstances, people or possessions that can have an influence over us. What is the effect of such a change of perspective? Instead of being influenced by circumstances, possessions or people, it becomes us, ourselves, who have an influence on circumstances, possessions or people, according to our positive qualities.

As a result of this new perspective, our mental state stops depending on what others say or do. Although we listen and accept their advice, in the end it is us, ourselves, who decide on and create our mental attitude.

When we are more aware of how we think and feel, we

recognise the most positive and beautiful features of our personality, but we are also aware of the negative habits that we have created, that manifest themselves in the form of fears, prejudices, addictions, and other unhappy states.

The first step, and one of the most important in order to free ourselves of those negative personality features, is to recognise them, and from there, to take the strong determination of wanting to transform that darkest part of our being.

To free ourselves of our dark places, we have to come out and apply, in our life, values such as trust, love and compassion. When the sun comes out, the darkness goes. As we allow our positive qualities and features to rule, the 'dark' tendencies will get progressively weaker. If we focus ourselves on our intrinsic, original and authentic qualities (peace, love and strength, amongst others), we accumulate more energy and our inner strength grows. This means that we are capable of creating and of having more strength of will, and, in this way, strengthening our self-esteem and achieving our aims.

The Power of the Other

We feel ourselves to be insignificant on experiencing the overwhelming power of the outer world. On feeling ourselves to be threatened by the power of the other, we can come to give up our individual integrity under the influence of the other and society. We use avoidance mechanisms in order to feel that the world stops being threatening. We stop being ourselves, taking on a personality that follows cultural and social norms. In this way, the discrepancy disappears between the 'I' and the world, and with it the fear of aloneness and impotence also disappears. We look for security, consolation and protection.

Being ourselves and different to others brings with it the risk of feeling alone. Fear dominates us. Following social, cultural, religious and political norms seems to offer us more security and feeds our feeling of belonging. On feeling that we form part of a group, whether it be a family, a team, a political party, a community or a spiritual or religious congregation, we make ourselves available to submitting ourselves to 'new' authorities, capable of offering us security and relieving us from doubt. This attitude feeds dependence and the loss of one's own freedom. In the section "dependencies" we will explore different dimensions of dependence.

When the other exercises power over us we react without being fully the owner of our emotions. Let us look at some examples:

Accept or Get Frustrated

In relation to the other, we have to be aware that there are two things in life that we can never change: the past and other people. This often brings us one frustration after the other, especially when we do not get the results that we want. Frustration is also a sign of failure, and every time that you fail in getting what you want from the other, your self-esteem and self-confidence are reduced.

Frustration is a form of anger. You allow emotion to control you, and therefore you lose control. You try to do the impossible: change what cannot be changed. Most times situations will not be as you want them to be and neither will people behave as you want them to. Therefore, you can decide now if you want to continue allowing the other to dictate your reactions according to how they behave, which results in the loss of your governance and personal power, or you can decide that no matter how the other behaves, you rule over your responses; you decide what you want to think and feel.

When another tries to control you and then gets frustrated because you don't do what he or she wants or you aren't who he or she expects you to be, they get in a bad mood with you; they look at you with anger and what do you do? You place a light barrier, invisible, between you and him or her. In such a way that they cannot 'enter' into your world and you do not leave yours either, they lose their influence over you. Paradoxically, when you try to control people you lose influence over them and distance is generated.

Control or Influence

The power of influence is extraordinary, but it practically disappears when we try to exercise control and force. You can influence positively in many ways: listening, encouraging, sharing, creating and communicating in the right way, in the right moment and situation. In control we generate stress, frustration and anger. In positive influence the energy flows in a relaxed way with harmony and is not threatening, allowing each one to be as they are. In order to influence positively we need a good capacity of discernment and clarity in the decisions that we take in relation to what to say and what to do.

The power of a clear intellect and discernment helps us in all situations. For example, when you believe that the other person is the problem; generally the problem is not what others say or do, but rather how you perceive them. The way that you judge is what creates your negative feelings about them. In fact, the real problem lies in how you see the other.

We have the choice to perceive others as a threat, as a problem, or as an opportunity; an opportunity for learning, for change, for dialogue and understanding. We can choose to have compassion; to feel that the other is a problem indicates a lack of compassion.

Conflict with the Other

Sometimes we feel that the other is not only a problem but also a source of conflicts. We have to be aware that there always have to be two people involved for there to be an unhappy or conflictive exchange. When we are in any conflict, it is difficult to see and understand the true causes and the real dynamic of the process of the conflict. The emotions that arise distract us and even blind us.

In the first place, it is important to recognise that your responsibility in any situation of conflict is your contribution to the conflict. The process of responding to any person or situation is something that takes place in you. Nothing can make you feel anything without your permission.

If you have been in conflict with someone for a time, for sure, you create fear or anger towards them, expressing thus behaviours of resistance when you communicate or relate to them. The other person is not responsible for your emotions or for your behaviour.

Your experience of conflict and your contribution to the conflict begin in your consciousness and you keep them in your consciousness. It begins with your perception of the other. If you perceive them negatively you will think negatively; you will feel negative and create a negative attitude; you will behave negatively, and so you will transmit a negative energy. You don't have to do it like that. Perception is a choice.

When there is conflict there is mental and emotional pain, even physical. Who creates that pain? You! Who creates at least half of the conflict? You! Where do you dissolve it? In your consciousness – in you. Seen like this, freeing yourself of the conflict is a matter of a decision. At any moment you can decide not to be in conflict. The resolution of the conflict can only begin with the dissolution of the conflict. One party has to dissolve their contribution to the conflict, even if it is temporarily, for the process of resolution to be able to begin.

In the second place, it is good to realise that the energy that you put into the conflict will possibly be the quality of energy that you will receive in return. This is the law of reciprocity. On a subtle level, we radiate according to our attitude, and on a physical level, we radiate according to our behaviour. What we transmit will return to us in a similar way; unless the 'other' is 'wiser' and decides not to give us back the same negative energy, but rather to treat us in exchange with a positive attitude and proactive behaviour. That way, that person won't stimulate dependence, but rather they will help us to free ourselves of our own negativity.

Often, conflict between two people happens because we do not get the result that we want; we are stuck to getting a specific result and we allow our happiness to depend on getting it or not. On not getting it, we use an erroneous method; we generate a conflict, we feel ourselves to be victims, we blame the other, we project our pain onto them; all of this under the belief that others – the other – is who makes us happy. This is a belief based on a mirage.

When your happiness depends on your expectations being fulfilled, it is difficult to be happy in a constant way. Often expectations are disguised desires, and where there are desires there is fear – the fear of not getting what you want. When you don't get it you get unhappy and, in so doing, you keep happiness away from you. It is good to set yourself goals, but if they are not fulfilled don't lose your sense of wellbeing. Your happiness is a much more valuable treasure than the external achievement of your expectations and of those that others have of you.

Being Impressed by the Other

Another aspect that we need to pay attention to is in relation to when the other impresses us. Being impressed, in itself, is not bad, but we can fall into the tendency of staying trapped in the superfluous and in appearances. What impresses us influences us and even moulds our awareness at that moment. We lose the ability to create our thoughts and feelings and these are influenced by the impression that we have allowed the other person to leave in us. Sometimes the impression is such that we abandon ourselves to it. We give up our power to the other, and we allow them to dominate our emotional world. The results of allowing oneself to be impressed are varied and on different levels.

For example, when we are impressed by the other's position;

it is fine to respect the authority and the position of the other, but when we allow their position to impress us, our ability to relate to the person in a fluid way is blocked. This can come to make it difficult for us to be the authority in our own life.

Another example is when we are impressed by the achievements of the other and put them on a pedestal. We compare ourselves with him or her and have weak thoughts of ourselves, such as that we are not as good or effective as them, or we might feel jealousy or guilt. All of this acts as an obstacle on the path towards our own achievement.

When we are impressed by the communication skills of another, we repress ourselves and we do not bring out to the light the best of ourselves. We become clumsier than we really are.

It is good to recognise and appreciate the achievements and skills of others, but when we allow them to impress us, in some way, we submit ourselves to their influence and we weaken our self-esteem and our respect towards ourselves. Without realising, we use the other to fill a gap or a lack that we feel in ourselves. This will not always work. It will not strengthen us; rather it will create a dependency and dependencies weaken us.

The Look of the Other

Another aspect to take into account is how much you are influenced by what you believe that others think of you and how they see you. The degree to which you act on the basis of what you think others want and expect of you, allows them to have power over your inner and outer world.

Important aspects are how you think others see you, how you want them to see you and how you see yourself. The person who is not conditioned by how others see them, and doesn't even think about how they would like to be seen, but who rather is comfortable with themselves, has a presence that generates comfort. Others feel fine around that person.

Let us learn to free ourselves from the conditionings that

generate the thinking of how we want others to see us. Let us feel the freedom to let ourselves be how we want to be.

Try it and you will see that the results are good. That way, as you go along, you will take off the masks that are brought about by the fears of what others will say and think.

Being an Actor and Being an Observer

In relation to the other, we have the possibility of observing and intervening when we wish to; that is, between being an observer and acting; playing between forming part of the audience and being the actor. On being actors, we can lose ourselves in the acting of the other in his or her or their dramas; we get in so deep with what is happening to the other that we lose distance. We get mentally and emotionally involved in the other's stories. When our awareness gets lost in those stories, we stop being the creators of our own life and of our own story. This habit exhausts us; we lose energy; we get dispersed and we lose control over our thoughts and our emotions. We lose our inner peace and we begin to look for it again.

Reality has different dimensions, and if we choose to live the reality of others, their stories and their complications, we lose our inner tranquillity. We can choose to observe the dance of ideas, images and acts of others, and not get involved in their stories. Only thus will we be at peace with ourselves and with the world. Remember that you create your own story. If you want to live in peace and exercise a positive influence, don't try to control or to change the stories of others.

In order to enjoy a painting you do not stick your nose onto it; you keep at a certain distance so you see it with greater clarity. The same thing occurs with life. By learning the art of observing and intervening, of keeping a healthy distance and of acting on the great work of life, we manage to be connected with what is essential without losing ourselves in the trivial and superfluous, and without losing ourselves in the stories of others. That way, our intervention does not arise out of a reaction coloured by frustration, anger and negative judgements. We are the creators of spaces of trust and love.

Pending Conversations

All of the matters, messages, ideas and feelings that you want to communicate and/or clear up with someone but you still haven't done, mean an inner burden that you sustain. To communicate the essential, and what has meaning to people that you love and are important for you, is an act of love and care. To leave pending and to postpone conversations means to accumulate things to say, matters to clear up and ideas to dialogue with, inside of you. It means a burden that prevents you from living the present with full freedom. You have something pending.

There are people who, only on the verge of death, hasten to say what they feel, to clarify matters and to communicate feelings. It seems that feeling death to be near gives them the courage to dare to open themselves and communicate that which they have wanted to say for so long but have put off.

In a seminar that I gave, Marta explained the burden that she felt for not having said to her mother, who had died three years before, how grateful she was and how sorry not to have asked her forgiveness for her behaviour towards her. She put off the conversation until it was too late and her mother died. After three years, Marta continued to feel that burden within.

What might have been, and was not, can no longer be fixed. We simply have to accept how the past happened and not live with regrets that increase our inner heaviness. We have to learn from it, not put off conversations, but clear up matters as they arise and not be afraid. We must create the necessary space to share in a safe atmosphere, protected from violence and full of respect. In that atmosphere, we can express ourselves, share and love. We have to create the atmosphere ourselves. It is our responsibility to make the other understand that there is something important that we have to tell them.

In order to live in freedom we have to be aware of all the burdens that we have pending from the past, what things we have to fix, solve, clear up and communicate, and free ourselves from all of them.

To start with, make a list of all the pending conversations that you have. Give yourself a date that is soon and realistic in order to have these conversations. Make them happen. Don't put them off any more.

Don't allow your mind to keep on making excuses. Imagine that today is your last day. What is it that you have to say, communicate, and/or clarify and with who? Do it soon. Today might be your last day or the last day of the person with whom you have a pending conversation.

Living without pending conversations keeps the path clear, your conscience clear and your heart at peace.

Dependencies

Attaching ourselves and depending are two habits that we have so deeply ingrained that they seem normal to us. On attaching ourselves, we create fears, amongst which the main one is the fear of loss. Fear, anger and sadness originate in the habits of latching on, attaching oneself and depending. With them our heart has lost freedom. The pressure that those emotional states generate and the absence of true freedom bring us suffering and even a state of feeling ourselves victims or miserable.

We are so accustomed to these forms of suffering that we come to believe that they are aspects of human nature and are, therefore, natural. And so we are prepared to pay the price of maintaining dependencies with stress, suffering and unhappiness to the point that some of us become ill. The natural state of the self is free and not trapped into dependencies. The suffering indicates to us that there is something not natural and abnormal. It is possible to stop suffering these emotional upsets. To do so we first have to understand our inner mechanisms. What happens when we become dependent and clinging?

When we cling-on to something we attach ourselves to the object that we are clutching on to. On saying 'object' I refer both to external things, such as people or places, and to internal things, such as ideas, beliefs or memories. However, the act of clinging on is always internal. For example, if you clutch onto and attach yourself to the armchair, you will say "my armchair". The armchair is an external object, but you hold on to it inside you – in your consciousness. You have an image of the armchair in your mind and you attach your being to the image in your mind. You are not your mind and neither are you what is in your mind. However, one of our most deeply-rooted habits is that of losing ourselves in what is in our mind; confusing the self with what is in our own mind. What is in the mind is always only an image or an idea.

Many times the attachment originates in a bad channelling of love. Love is the energy that inspires us, motivates us, moves us, embraces us and opens us to embrace life. What is paradoxical is that many dependencies begin with this energy, the most powerful – love. The energy of love is a magnet that has a lot of power. When you love someone there is a magnet that attracts you and keeps you connected to that person, but the moment that the love turns into a dependency and into attachment, freedom is lost. Is it possible to love and be free? Or, when we love do we automatically trap ourselves and become dependent?

When you add attachment and dependency to love, that love will not be healing, because there will be expectations in it. Unconditional love is healing, and never wounds. When love is mixed with a desire for possession and attachment, you want to control the other. From this control, you exercise a power over them which means they are under submission or influence. That way, you feel that you have them and that they belong to you. In this kind of relationship there is pain.

When the people that love you begin to feel that they possess you, you do not feel free, but rather controlled. It is one thing for someone to look out for you and care for you out of love. However it is a very different thing for them to control and dominate you.

If someone gets angry with you and manages to make you react and get upset, they dominate you. They know that, when they want to control you, what they should do is to get angry with you and that way they will achieve it. When you react you are allowing this control. It is you that chooses to allow yourself to be influenced and dominated. It is important for us to realise that we can choose and take the decision to allow ourselves to be controlled and dominated, or we can choose to express what we feel without being affected by the reaction of the other and maintaining respect.

Let us not allow ourselves to be dominated by external objects, or we will lose energy. So many influences from the past, from others, from fear and anxieties, cause us to wilt. We have disconnected from the root and from the seed. The seed is divine energy. The roots are our values that connect us to our seeds, to our origins, to what really matters, to what is authentic and essential. When you are connected to the roots, a marvellous plant grows and your beauty emerges. You are unique, you are different.

Each one of us is different. Each flower is unique. When you like a flower a lot, you pick it; you want it for yourself. But, what happens to the flower? It wilts. Sometimes we do this with people. We like a person, we get close to them, we stick ourselves onto them and we absorb their energy; we trap them and we don't allow them the necessary space to grow and develop fully and openly. The challenge is to know how to love and be free at the same time; to learn to love, maintaining respect and freedom in such a way that, in this love, you feel free and the other does too. The reality is that you cannot possess anybody and, therefore, neither can you lose them. To feel a loss arises out of living out the mirage of possession.

If we ask ourselves who has caused us the most suffering in life, it will possibly be those who we most love or have loved. It happens like that because we believe that the energy of love will come from the outside and will fill our inner void. We haven't cultivated our spirituality. Due to our lackings we cling to the person or the object of our love, believing that they will fill us, and, as it does not always happen like that, we suffer.

In a seminar I asked what the moments of greatest fullness have been and two or three people answered that it was the birth of their children. The child does not give you anything and yet it gives you everything. What does it give you? The opportunity to love him or her unconditionally. Their presence in your life offers you tenderness, their affection, and it opens you to the affection you have inside and gives you the opportunity to express it. They re-connect you with innocence, they disconnect you from the complications of rational analysis, they calm your mind, they connect you to the world of imagination and they present you with existential questions that remind you of what is essential.

Love is an energy that goes from the inside out, and, when it comes out of that clean, free and silent place that rises up within you, it has the healing, energising and creative power to open the other to receive and give the best of themselves.

We have an inner void because we are disconnected from our true being and we think that the energy of love will come from the outside to fill us. Then we open ourselves to the possibility of depending. Depending, on the outside, creates the vacuuming effect: when you vacuum to clean, you suck up the good and the bad. If you have dropped an earring or a ring, the vacuum cleaner takes it away, together with the dust and the dirt. When you live with the vacuuming effect to suck up the love of the other, to suck up the affection of the other, the care of the other, their strength or their energy, you also end up sucking in their weaknesses, their doubts and their fears. That way, a dependency is generated that causes pain.

Clinging-on Causes Unhappiness

In not clinging is the willingness to flow freely and to enjoy and to taste and to relish each new instant of life.
Anthony de Mello

The life that Anthony de Mello speaks of is sweeter now, because it has been freed of tension and insecurity; free of the fear of loss and of death that also accompanies the desire to stay and cling-on.

These days it is difficult to find a happy person, given that many people are hooked onto something. They cling-on to money, to the past, the future, power, success, failure, fears, people, objects, beliefs, their ideologies, the system.

If our heart is attached, that is, if it depends on someone or something, it will be impossible to experience true enjoyment and happiness. When we are attached to something or to someone, it means that our mind and heart are taken up with our attachments, making sure that they 'are near', and often we get lost in them. In this state of consciousness we cannot stay open to the new opportunities that come into our lives; in fact, we are blocking them.

When you are hooked, you are not free and you suffer. You become a victim. The sign that there is egotism, dependence or attachment, is that you suffer. In the measure that you become unhooked, you free yourself, you become unblocked, you get back freedom and happiness.

Our habits of clinging-on and of worrying ourselves are so strong that we need an extra strength that helps us to detach ourselves and free us. Meditation helps us to connect to that 'extra' energy and strength.

Clinging-on is a sign of insecurity and low self-esteem. When we have a great lack of confidence in ourselves, we get attached. When this happens, we allow other people and situations to dominate our mind and our heart. In doing this we renounce the most precious thing that we have as human beings: freedom – the capacity for creativity and choice. We give the power to situations or people to dominate our choice – what we think, say and do.

Attachments and dependencies, fears and insecurity, block our experience of love, of peace, of serenity, freedom and happiness. When you have a feeling of love that leads you to enjoyment, to wholeness, and then you attach yourself to the object of your love (a person, a property, a dog, etc.); automatically, the feeling is centred on fear: you fear to lose the object of your love and, instead of experiencing wholeness and happiness, you experience fear. Your thoughts are in function of what you depend on, so that there is not wholeness; rather you start becoming empty within and your energy level goes down.

Opening Oneself to Receive Help

Some dependencies are necessary, and we have to accept them. For example, if someone is ill and very, very weak, they need to be cared for. Although there are people who are so independent and autonomous that they do not accept the love that being cared for implies. That help that is more constant for some, due to physical reasons, is, from time to time, when they are ill, necessary.

We depend on oxygen, given that it is necessary to live. We live thanks to the fact that the lungs do their work of inhaling and exhaling almost without our realising and, when this does not happen, the body stops working. There are people who, when sleeping, experience apnoea – they stop breathing for a few seconds and then they wake up – so that, in order to sleep safely and rest well, they come to depend on a machine, which is also a necessary dependence.

By this, I mean that not all dependencies are bad. There are all kinds of dependencies in life and it is important to be aware of what power they exercise over us – what influence they have in our life. A person who does not allow them self to be cared for when ill, can end up worse if they do not accept that help. The need for help opens us up to tenderness and love; it allows us to receive. It makes possible a relationship of another kind with the person who is there to help us.

Expecting Special Treatment

Sometimes, we get ill almost on purpose in order to receive special treatment. Out of a lack of self-esteem and insecurity, we depend on the appreciation and affection of the other, for them to value us, praise us and always to speak kindly to us. Even though they have given us many signs of appreciation, if for a few days they give us none, our inner world or our self-esteem collapses. We become dependent on what others do, or don't do, in relation to us, whether or not they nourish our self-esteem, and then what happens? We are always waiting for the other to give us something when in reality we can give it to ourselves.

Depending on How Others See You

Watch how many things you do during the day are dependent on how you imagine the other sees you: your husband, your friend, your child, your cousin, your aunt, your boss, the secretary or whoever. You imagine how they are going to look at you and, as a consequence, you project. If you depend on the look of the other, inwardly you will always feel fear. You want to please the other so that they continue to see you as you want.

Because of the dependence that we have on the other to appreciate us, value us and not to reject us, we want to please them. If, in spite of doing everything possible, they do not appreciate us or are not happy, how do we feel? Cheated. After having done everything out of wanting to please them!

At bottom, you want to please them because you want them to keep on loving you, or you don't want them to sack you from your job, or you are afraid of being different or not being accepted. That kind of dependency takes us away from our true authenticity. If you look at yourself well, in the end, others will look at you well and the one who does not look at you well will perhaps teach you something, but your value and self-esteem do not depend on the look of the other. In this state, you are open because you trust in yourself and you have personal security.

The other can also be God. We are afraid that God might judge us for being sinners or not. If God looks at me with that vision of whether I am a sinner, whether I am thus or something else, I distance myself from Him. A judge like that does not help me to live with wholeness. In general, in society, there has been a distancing from the relationship and experience with God, because we have learned that He is a repressive being and a judge. For me, God is love; God looks at me well and sees my potential and my beauty (which reflects His), God embraces me and, in this embrace, He frees me: He does not allow me to depend on Him.

Depending on an External Stimulus in Order to be Happy

Sometimes we depend on external entertainment – for others to entertain us – because, if not, we get bored. We need to escape from ourselves, relax, forget or disconnect; for example, watching television or playing computer games. However, there are many other things that we could be doing, which are more beneficial, positive and creative.

The dependence on being entertained increases mental laziness. Personal creativity atrophies and we consume more external entertainment, generating the addiction to being stimulated from the outside.

When you need an external stimulus in order to bring about certain emotional states, you keep up dependence. For example, if you like to argue because it makes you feel energetic, in reality you are using anger. Or if you keep on talking about what went wrong or what you lost, you are wallowing in your grief and sorrows.

Do you remember the first time that they took you to the circus? Mum or dad asks us: "Is it fun? Are you having a good time? Are you happy? Isn't it great?" And, thus, they taught us two lessons: that fun and emotion are the same as happiness and that what we feel in life has to come from outside.

Excitement and emotion are like what happens to water when it boils. It is agitation, not happiness, for the human being. Happiness is satisfaction; it is wholeness, and a constant flow of joy. Being excited is not the same as happiness. It is a passing emotional state. Happiness is permanent, with solid internal bases. In happiness you feel satisfied, peaceful and whole.

If you believe that your feelings come from outside, what are you going to do for the rest of your life? Look for something outside that makes you feel something inside? This is called stimulation. On believing that your feelings have to come from outside, you depend on something in order to feel: a person, a place, an object, a substance, a football team.

Sometimes, when we arrive home after a busy day, we need to relax. And we switch on the television to see the film of the night: *Rambo III* – ninety minutes of fear, horror, blood and violence. And what will we do, relax or be stimulated? Stimulated.

The experts in marketing have been astute; they have convinced us that stimulation is relaxation and we have all become addicted to something. What are we doing? We are depending on someone or something external in order to be happy; confusing our happiness with something that is on the outside. We haven't learned to create and feel happy from the inside; therefore, we have to be stimulated. This, in reality, makes us suffer. There is only one way to begin to change it: admit to the addiction.

Being fully awake is to have broken the dependence on emotional stimulation from the outside in. An awoken being has learned to choose and to create his or her feelings in each moment and at each scene, regardless of the external stimuli.

Depending on Novelty and Going Shopping

One of the dependencies that the consumer society promotes is that of the new. You have a car but today a new, better one is coming out. You have a mobile but the new one on the market today has more features and yours is now obsolete. The same thing happens to the television, personal stereos (MP3), the video (DVD), etc. Today you have some clothes but tomorrow the fashion will be different. We need to fill ourselves more and more. This way an addiction to the new is generated. We get bored quickly and we need something apparently new and different.

On a radio programme that I participate in, one day we talked about the addiction to the new. A man called in, telling us the following: "Every week my wife needs to buy new clothes because it makes her feel better, she feels the newness, is it normal?" I thought that perhaps she would have to hire a warehouse to use as a cupboard to keep all the clothes in. But, meanwhile, there are people in other parts of the world who don't even have a jacket to put on. I told the man that it is the addiction to the new out of boredom, discomfort with oneself, and the need to impress and please another that so many people share. It is to spend without responsibility. It is to live in the superficiality 'of the suit', not in the essence of being. It is to use time to distract oneself and not to construct creatively. If you felt death to be near, and these were your last days, you would devote yourself to something more essential and significant.

A mother rang into the programme expressing her concern because, on the market, there always appears the novelty of the same product wrapped differently. There always seems to be a new Coca Cola, a new kind of yoghurt, but they are really the same products as always. The only thing that changes is the packaging and their image. Her children, whenever they go to the supermarket, want the new kinds of biscuits, yoghurt, etc. They always want new things that then stay in the fridge and the woman asks herself what to do. We teach little ones by telling them that happiness is stimulation, the new is stimulating, and comes from the outside or you get it from the outside. We create an addiction to the new; in this case, to the newness of the packaging. What kind of newness is that!

When, in order to be happy, you need to go shopping, you try to fill yourself with something that isn't you. You try to find wholeness by filling your life with things. A being that is awake knows that they are already complete and can never be diminished. The only effort is in remembering and reconnecting with their whole self, their complete self.

Dependence on Fame and Power

Aspiring to be famous causes continuous stress and anxiety. You participate in a race in which you compete and are comparing yourself constantly. You stop taking care of yourself and nourishing your being. You take care of your image but not your soul. This brings about an inner void and loneliness that, sometimes, is unbearable for us.

Reaching fame, financial wealth, the power of a visible position, and reaching it with a broken soul, a broken apart family and a sick body, causes depression.

A concert pianist once told me that, in the world of music and piano players, if you give a hundred concerts a year you are better and you are more. A time arrived when she said to herself "This is stressful. Is this what I want? More than a hundred concerts a year to be at the top of the range, so that then they invite you to the best places. No, I want to share music, but in another way, without stress, without fighting to reach and maintain fame and power."

I offer this example because she revised her purpose: "What do I want? Why do I do what I do? For what and for who do I do it? What is the price that I have to pay for this dependence on fame?"

Repetitive Thoughts

There are mental dependences that arise out of a badly channelled imagination, false beliefs or mental weakness. For example, this happens when the pattern of negative thoughts makes us wallow in feelings of guilt. Or we think, almost obsessively, that someone wants to hurt us or are after us. They are negative and self-destructive habits. We fall into repetitive thoughts, which lead us to live in constant unhappiness.

We spend a lot of time during the day with unnecessary thoughts. They are leaks of energy that weaken us and bring unhappiness. We have created the habit of thinking like that and, therefore, it is in our hands to learn to transform it. We can free ourselves of these dependencies and the result is to be freer, mentally, of negative and repetitive thoughts, which are like a constant hammering. It is a question of learning to control what we think, thinking positively, meditating and exercising the mind. We exercise to keep the body healthy and strong; in order to have a healthy and strong mind we have to learn exercises that help us to free ourselves from the bad positions of the mind.

How do we get Hooked?

We have to dare to be free. Why? Because fear prevents us from taking the decisions that lead us to live and feel our full freedom. We should dare to let go because dependencies trap us. Let us look at a story that shows us what happens.

It is the story of a bird that, after having flown for a long time, leans on the branch of a tree to rest. While resting, it finds the wellbeing of staying there until, little by little, it gets the idea that its life is on the branch. When a day arrives on which it asks itself why it doesn't carry on flying, it says "Oh, this branch is stuck to me and I can't fly!" The bird blames the branch. In reality, the bird has got stuck to the branch. It has the capacity and the wings to fly but its perception has clouded over. It no longer sees its purpose with clarity or its potential to reach it. The freedom of the bird is in its wings but it has got stuck onto the branch. That is the reality that it has created for itself.

The freedom of the human being is in his or her awareness. But when their awareness has got stuck onto the branch (the object of their attachment) and they begin to blame the branch for their impossibility to free themselves, then they are trapped. When our awareness is clouded over and clinging-on, we do not see with clarity and neither do we exercise our freedom.

Another example is that of the monkey; you can trap a monkey by giving it a jar with peanuts in it. The monkey puts its hand in the jar to get the peanuts. On having its hand full of peanuts it can't get it out of the jar, so you have trapped it. To free itself the only thing it has to do is let go of the peanuts and that way it will be able to take its hand out. That is how we are at times, like monkeys; we don't let go and we stay trapped in situations, in people, in the past.

Along the way, we will find a lot of jars with peanuts in and branches to settle down on – many scenes that will attract us and please us. The dependency begins, almost without our realising, when we begin to feel the desire to be in these situations. The pleasure turns into desire, the desire turns into need and the need turns into habit, then to addiction and finally into a dependence. It is fine to enjoy the branches, but let us keep awake and alert – conscious of our freedom – in order not to fall into dependence; enjoying the branch without it trapping us.

An example of how this process takes place can be seen in some smokers. The smoker, little by little, liked smoking, then desired to smoke, then needed to smoke; he/she created the habit of smoking, it turned into a dependence and finally into an addiction. It began because he liked it but it ended up generating that addiction.

We live disconnected from ourselves, with a lot of unnecessary dependencies and needs. When you think that you need to smoke, you believe something that is not true. What does it mean that you need to smoke? Your body is delighted not to be a living chimney; we already breathe in enough pollution from cars without breathing in more unnecessary smoke. However, the person who smokes believes that it is a need and, while they believe it, they don't realise, or if they do realise, they don't want to accept that it is an unnecessary dependence.

This process can happen in many other contexts: emotional, mental and physical dependencies and addictions towards people, objects and ideas. When we are hooked we lose emotional, mental and intellectual agility in our being and in our awareness. The solution is in knowing how to let go.

Letting Go

Daring to be free is to dare to let go of the branches, which does not mean to lose them because the branches are always there. You can return to them to rest or to pause on the road. It is about being attentive, aware and awake, because the moment that pause turns into a stop, the stop turns into a brake and, after that, the brake turns into a blockage. As a result, your mental, intellectual and emotional agility starts to atrophy.

When we can see, and clearly understand, the suffering brought about by dependencies and attachment, we can recognise the essential need to detach oneself. When you hang onto something, in some way, you flatten, repress and diminish your own being. Your potential for creative energy is reduced or dormant. Realising that clinging-on is self-destructive, and that attachment is a form of spiritual suicide, is the key to beginning the practice of detachment. To detach yourself does not mean to stop caring or to have an uncaring attitude. It does not mean to be cold or dry. In order to free ourselves of all mental and emotional suffering we need to practise it.

To overcome the fear of loss that we associate with detachment, it is useful to nurture the truth that possession is a mirage. From a spiritual point of view, it is not possible to possess anything. All life comes and it goes. Hanging on to anything is useless; a waste of time and energy. If we can come to realise this, we will be very close to experiencing happiness, enjoyment and the joy of living in freedom.

Freeing oneself from suffering is not achieved with the desire to be free, which is a form of hanging onto a concept of freedom. Freedom comes with the end of clinging-on. It means to separate oneself or to stop identifying with the image of the object that one is attached to. We should remember that, by an object, I am referring to something external, such as things, people or places, or something internal, such as ideas, beliefs or memories.

We need the courage to let go of our attachments, above all, on a mental and emotional level. It is a question of strengthening the courage to maintain our detachment especially when external pressures (generally other people) and inner forces (our personal habits) incite us to cling-on – to depend and attach ourselves again.

When we learn to let go we realise that it is the road towards true freedom. We recognise to what point we had attached ourselves and depended. When someone stops depending and attaching themselves, they don't cling to anything, not even to ideas, histories, situations, possessions, habits or personality traits. They find themselves in an open space; an inner space without barriers, without limits, without objects. In that space there is peace. You are aware of the connection of all things. In that space there lives love, and from it love emerges and is expressed.

You realise that the happiness and tranquillity that seemed to come from our dependences can only be temporary and often superficial. Between those moments of induced happiness, there is fear.

To see and understand this process of attachment you need a state of being that is aware, to be attentive and alert. The practice of meditation opens the doors to that state to us, because it quietens the mind and opens the heart.

Worried minds and closed hearts make it difficult to see and receive new ideas, opportunities and even people in our life. In a true state of awareness of being we free ourselves of the anchors of attachment. When we recognise ourselves as spiritual beings, we can forget many conditionings and false concepts about being that have made up part of our education. In doing so, we lose nothing. On the contrary, we rediscover our real and authentic being. We control our inner world and the access to our spiritual power.

Listening to our intuition will help us. It is the voice connected to the authenticity of your being. It is the voice of the soul. If you listen, intuition will remind you that you are free. You came naked to this world, with nothing, and you will go naked, with nothing. During your life you go along collecting things, objects and people that you get hooked onto, and then you will cry because you will have to leave them or they will leave you. We live the journey of life, but we come naked and we go naked. Let's live in the essential.

With meditation we empty ourselves of all the accumulated loads, of the useless and superfluous, of the non-harmonious noises of thought. On emptying ourselves of all that is unnecessary, finally we welcome in the essential and we feel whole.

Creativity and Positive Thinking

As well as learning to let go, the correct use of creativity and positive thinking helps us to overcome dependencies. Often we live under the illusion that we can only be happy thanks to objects, people and places, but happiness is something that we experience when we put our heart into something, and our intention is of giving and not of taking. In the creative activity that we experience greatest enjoyment in, our happiness comes from within and expresses itself outwards, and not from the outside in.

Creative personal development helps us to overcome laziness.

On overcoming it, we recover the inner strength necessary to free ourselves of certain dependencies, such as the dependency on the creativity of others to entertain us. It is fine to enjoy entertainment, but the important thing is that you are capable of spending a good amount of time being creative yourself, overcoming laziness, boredom and inner creative atrophy.

With your thoughts and feelings you create and perceive the world that surrounds you. According to what your thoughts are, thus will be your feelings and emotions, your attitude and your actions. This process usually happens rapidly, and you are not usually aware that it is taking place. As this process repeats itself often, it is easy for a set of habits to be created.

The effort lies in slowing down this process in the mind, as if you were watching television in slow motion. On the screen of your consciousness you can use meditation as a method to slow down all this process and be aware of what you are feeling and thinking, how you are acting and being aware of the result that you obtain.

It is important to learn to transform and come to avoid, that is, to not create unnecessary thoughts in order to be more centred and energised, and to have more clarity in order to take the right decisions.

Positive thoughts heal and strengthen the mind. A healthy mind is the basis of a balanced personality.

Let us learn to create thoughts of greater quality. They arise out of a wider vision of our inner being. In this way, thanks to those positive thoughts, full of peace, harmony and creativity, the mind will clean itself, and the memory of our innate qualities will be activated once more, replacing, in a natural way, the old habits and negative tendencies.

Trust

We have to trust that, being ourselves, we will be well-received and loved by the world. If we are here, why have we been incarnated on Earth? To satisfy the look of the other or to bring what is unique and exceptional in us? We all have two eyes, a nose and a mouth but no face is the same. We are all a being of conscious energy but each one has a colour, an art, a creativity and something different to contribute. Let us trust in ourselves and use our talents to bring our difference.

You can be your best friend. Imagine that someone accompanies you in your life, values everything that you do and finds it to be great: what you do, what you say; you are the best; extraordinary; a shining being; a star.

Now imagine that you have that person next to you day and night. How do you feel? On top form and you are fine. This happens when you fall in love. When someone falls in love with you, they practically only think about you; they ring you, they send you text messages, maybe they write you letters. They are wrapped up in you. You feel unique, special and loved. But this does not last forever and, nowadays, it lasts less and less. The difficulty is that if you depend on the look of the other to feel fine, sometimes you will be fine if chance has it that the person looking at you does it well, but if not, you won't be fine.

How do you look at yourself? This unconditional friend that loves you so much and that supports you is what you have inside. You can be your best friend. This gives you security and trust. If someone else likes you or doesn't like you and criticises you, you won't collapse within because to be fine you do not depend on the look of the other.

Feeling Yourself to be a Victim or a Transforming Agent

Often, we feel ourselves to be victims of a complex reality in which there are different factors that seem to direct the course of our life without us being able to control them. The Universe does not seem to dance to our music and our will, and we feel ourselves to be victims because things do not work out or are not as we want. Therefore, we decide to resign ourselves to this reality; to be victims of it and observe passively, resisting what comes, getting frustrated and bad-tempered. However, we could position ourselves in another way: being transforming agents by creating a different reality. To do so we have to change our perception. Also, it is necessary to strengthen our capacity to tolerate, accept, let go and forget. Tolerance implies understanding, love and compassion. Not to put up with things, but to transcend them; to co-operate with trust and motivation. It is difficult for us to tolerate because we have expectations and pre-conceived ideas of how others should act and be. Then we create bad feelings towards them because they are not like that. This makes our relationship with them difficult.

When your vision towards others is positive, you see their qualities, their efforts and their values instead of their defects and their errors. You are open to listening to them and to understanding their intentions. That way it is easier to have good feelings towards them. Basing ourselves on a positive and objective vision and on good feelings, we do not have to put up with, or even tolerate, the other, given that the relationship is good.

If you go inside yourself and observe, with sincerity, your feelings towards someone that you consider 'unbearable', you will see that your perception, your projection, your expectations and your bad feelings make you feel that the other is 'unbearable'. You have allowed the other to influence you in the creation of your bad feelings. You have lost compassion and the capacity to accept and understand the other.

Being a transforming agent requires having full control over your inner world. If you are the victim of your rapidly moving mind, your bad feelings, your aggressive emotional states and of your not-very-healthy habits, you will easily feel yourself to be the victim of others, of circumstances, of time and of society.

The key is in living with your consciousness awake and not to do anything that your conscience does not agree with. You don't have to fear the opinion of others. You don't have to feel insecure or doubt yourself. If not, we will continue to act against our own consciousness and we will feel ourselves to be victims.

To avoid pain or the unhappiness that arises automatically when we act against our own consciousness, we look for guilty parties: "Because of... I haven't acted as I should." We blame or we make excuses. That way we keep down the voice of our consciousness until the suffering and unhappiness is such that our conscience shouts at us, as in the picture, The Scream, by Edvard Munch.

Yesterday is Already Past (Living Through Mourning)

Living trapped in the memory of a loved one who left us, or in the memory of a situation that no longer exists, or in the memory of someone who is alive but who we no longer see (since we have physically separated), does not allow us to enjoy the present moment with freedom.

Living through the mourning is the capacity to make peace with the memories recorded on our memory. It is to reach a point where they do not upset us or cause us pain. It is to acknowledge that the memory of what was and no longer is, no longer generates desires, dissatisfaction, frustration or sadness.

You don't get over the mourning of a loved one, a lost child, a disappeared love, because you allow the memory to continue alive, in a way that it invades the consciousness and colonises the spirit. The memory suffocates the present, wanting to relive a past that no longer has the possibility of existing. It finished.

To mourn is to free oneself of the known and lived. It is to cut the strings or ties of the attachment to this experience that has passed.

The dimension of mourning has different expressions and forms in relation to death. Judeo-Christian mourning is not like the Hindu. Judeo-Christian mourning is linked to the end of something. Hindu mourning is linked to the passing to another state. With the philosophy of reincarnation, mourning is made of a state, not a being.

In mourning, regret or remorse may emerge. Let's look at some feelings that are born in relation to these questions:

Did I do everything I should have?
Could I have avoided it?
Did I tell them everything I had to tell them?
Did I give them everything that they needed?
Was I there when they needed me?

These questions converge into a feeling of the responsibility of the death of the other. It is a mourning difficult to overcome. It requires an inner control that does not allow these questions and their answers to go on for a long time. If we don't achieve this capacity we fall into a regret for what might have been and was not, and the present escapes before our very eyes.

Mourning in relation to the separation from someone with whom you have shared moments of beauty and wholeness, of love and falling in love, requires an effort of serene acceptance. Not to remain trapped in feelings of guilt, bitterness or hate, given that they anchor us in a past that is no longer alive except in our consciousness, because we don't allow it to die. The images and memories of experiences of the past emerge again and again onto the screen of the mind, causing different kinds of feelings that range from sadness to frustration.

How quickly could a person get over the loss of a loved one and begin to feel fine? We have the capacity to do it the same day or the next day. But our beliefs and conditioning, our attachments and lack of will and inner capacity, prevent us from getting better rapidly and feeling fine.

Independently of the kind of mourning that you have to go through, it is a matter of preventing your memories from invading your spirit, your mind and your heart. Circumscribe them, limit them and put them in their place: in the past. Yesterday has already passed.

On the level of action, now, in the present, use your time, your talents and your thoughts for creative tasks. Help your neighbour. It will help you to come out of your aloneness and to relate. Share, dialogue and involve yourself in serving.

With respect to your accumulated experiences, meditate to gain mastery in managing your memories. Clean out the cupboards of your being, so that the stored memories do not cause upsets, interference or suffering in the present moment. Meditate to accept and let go.

Give thanks to the past. Learn from it. But now let go and free yourself. Live this moment in wholeness. It depends on you to create the right thought for it to be like that.

Freedom in Aloneness and in Shared Living

In Europe there are more and more people who live alone out of personal choice. Perhaps the choice to live alone comes after having experiences of pain, anguish and disappointment when living together in one or various relationships. Perhaps it is the search for freedom, peace and tranquillity that leads them to make this decision. That way you can do what you want, when you want and without having to explain yourself to anyone.

Are we made to live together or to live alone? Each human being has the need to belong. You can belong to a family, a group of friends, some trusted work partners, some colleagues, a spiritual or religious community, etc. The presence, participation and collaboration with others manages to inspire and challenge us to an extent that is inaccessible for a being on its own. True power and inner power is held by those who live and work together, not those who distance themselves from others. Because of others we do things that we wouldn't do for ourselves. That way, we widen our limits and make our heart bigger.

Each human heart is a potential source of love. Love is not

possible unless there is some kind of unity or mutual belonging. Ruptures, distancing or isolating oneself implies an absence of love and a lack of opportunities to give, express, share and love.

The challenge lies in loving and being loved, at the same time as allowing the other to be and being yourself too. In other words, loving and being free without feeling controlled or being controlling, without dependencies and without invading or feeling oneself invaded.

In order to live this love in freedom we require a strong heart; a heart free of dependencies; a heart free of selfish desires; a centred heart that knows that it cannot be wounded without its authorisation; a heart that does not submit itself to influences that break it or flatten it, but only to the divine influence that helps it to transcend and love from the centre of being, with the purest love.

In all religious and spiritual traditions it is considered that, to achieve this state of pure love, one has to reach maximum freedom, which is the freedom from the ego; transcending the individual 'I' in order to experience true communion with the divine, with God, with the other and with humanity.

The person who feels them self to be a pilgrim and attracted to the highest path sooner or later will feel organically that it is appropriate to commit themselves to some path. This means to participate in a spiritual community. Many spiritually motivated people, perhaps, feel a certain dislike towards groups and keep a distance from them, given that, at the end of the day, it is easier to work it out alone and do as you please.

The link between spiritual development and the process of growth in a group is clear. For the isolated and solitary person, growth is limited, since the personality is not activated in the same measure as when it interacts with others. In relationships and in shared living the defences of the ego and the games of the personality are stimulated, creating the possibility of being aware, of realising, and, therefore, of a greater growth and personal development.

In shared living we become aware of our egos. Because the egos bounce off each other, they suffer and blame. The egos control, dominate and pester. The egos desire and are constantly dissatisfied. If you are alone you don't become aware of the dimensions of your ego and, therefore, you cannot transcend it. You think you are you, but many times it is your ego that rules in your life, not you. When you are alone you do not realise this.

On living together, you have to practise all your qualities and inner powers: tolerance, the capacity to adapt, listen, understand, adjust, forgive, communicate, flow, discern, not be influenced, not depend, learn to be yourself living together with and being amongst others. Not to be you when you are alone and "another" when you are with others.

In India it is surprising to see the living together of multitudes. I have travelled a lot there by train. On one seat for three people there sit eight or ten. In a cabin for six, there are eighteen, and it seems not to bother them. When the inner space of being is cultivated, when you are conscious of the fact that nobody can take away what you are or your inner qualities, you can be amongst many, like on a train from Delhi to Mumbai (a whole day and night), and not feel that you have to defend a space.

In the West we are more accustomed to defending and moving in a physically defined individual space. But we forget that the important space to know, connect to, and define is the inner space. You feel comfortable and tranquil amongst other people when you are connected to the essential, to your authenticity. From that space you connect to the authenticity of others. It is an encounter of being to being, without defences.

The ego tries to defend 'its properties', its spaces. However, when you make yourself naked and you take off the defences of the ego you don't need to defend anything. What you are, you are. Nobody can take it away from you or destroy it.

The main obstacle towards true freedom and enlightenment is

your own ego. In order to 'flatten it' and transcend it, religious and spiritual communities advise obedience: obedience to some principles, writings, commandments, a guru, a priest, a shaman, a bishop, a teacher, a religious mother or father.

There we touch on another important question which is asked by any pilgrim who wants to go towards liberation. Being obedient, am I free? Where is my true freedom if I have to obey another or others or obey some principles, rules or systems? If I don't obey, is it my ego that does not obey? Can I be free and selfish at the same time? Is the liberation of the ego a greater and more authentic freedom than when I allow the ego to be free and to act, dominate and rule in my life? How much sacrifice does it require to liberate oneself from the ego in order to reach liberation and enlightenment?

Everyone should discover and find the answer to these questions. The difficulty is that, while our intellect is influenced and ruled by the ego or by certain selfish influences, the answers will come to us tainted and we won't be able to discern where or what authentic wisdom is. They will be answers of the ego in order to satisfy the ego itself, and that way we will continue to live in ignorance.

Meditation, silencing the mind, going into the sacred and silent inner space, helps our intellect to recover the power to discern what is authentic; differentiating it from what is false, discerning what is essential by differentiating it from the trivial or superficial.

Obeying certain principles, norms or disciplines in order to help us to control and finally free ourselves of certain selfish, materialist, sensual and/or emotional impulses, in the middle or long term, should lead us to an experience of being and a liberation in which we transcend even the need for those norms or disciplines.

Mahatma Gandhi practised discipline rigorously in the last stage of his life. He said to us, "If in the present day there are so many lies in our lost world it is because each one of the human beings claims the rights to an illuminated awareness without submitting themselves to any discipline at all."

The pilgrim who goes towards liberation, if he follows a path that connects to him and awakens the authentic in his being, will go through three stages: He will begin by learning to control and govern the instincts and basic and sensorial impulses dominated by the ego and all its ramifications (desires, greed, pride, arrogance, attachment, lust, anger, fear, laziness).

The second stage is about connecting to the sacred self; the true irreducible, indestructible, eternal self; the soul in its original state; luminous, with all its qualities, virtues and powers. Finally, in the third stage, the individual self is transcended to connect to God, live in unity, connected to others, the world and the Universe. In this transcendence the self is not annihilated, but with the selfish defences dissolved, the being is open to communion with others, without barriers or fears.

This process implies going towards the depth and, at the same time, going towards the beyond; transcending towards the Light – towards God. It is to go into the central space of the heart of being – the sacred inner temple – and transcending in ecstasy, joy and the union with God. Both steps, towards within and towards the unlimited, bring us closer to true wholeness.

In the first stage, the person focuses on containing, dominating and ruling over their most physical and sensorial impulses, and acquiring mental discipline. When they control them, they can focus on expanding and expressing their true being. That control implies understanding, comprehension and transcendence. It cannot take place through repression or force. Repression leads us to illness, and to the denaturalisation of the necessary process to reach true enlightenment where the being is authentic, is love, and is free.

To enter into the first stage, one prepares oneself to go through an apprenticeship that helps to achieve inner dominion. In this first phase, religious and spiritual paths propose the following of some moral codes that have no other finality than that of marking limits of the ego and helping to transcend it. There are many similarities amongst them. Let us see some examples:

In the Hebrew Decalogue, a contention is proposed of the primary instincts that can also be understood as a pedagogy of desire. After the three commandments dedicated to God, which put in the first place the absolute of God, the fourth refers to the respect and gratitude towards one's ancestors, those from whom life comes. To respect them is to remember that life is no possession, but rather a received gift that is transmitted from generation to generation. The fifth commandment is not to kill. It refers to controlling anger. The sixth and ninth commandments refer to the sexual impulse, another of the great vital forces that have to be learned to be controlled. The seventh commandment (not to steal) and the tenth (not to covet that of others) refer to the control of greed, envy; the sources of anxieties and upsets in both the area of interpersonal relationships and amongst nations. The eighth commandment (not to lie) defends the authenticity of the word and of life itself.

In the Koran we find a pedagogy devoted to controlling and transcending the desires of the ego itself. Idolatry is condemned. There is no other god except God. Only a God that is transcendent of our own desires will be capable of avoiding that we stay trapped in them. We should not go over our own limits if they invade those of others. The Koran recommends not being ambitious or selfish, but fair, true, pacific, humble and sincere.

In the practice of yoga we also find the importance of containing the impulses of the human being. According to the classical system of Patanjali, there are proposed five yama or necessary and previous renunciations for all spiritual practice: non-violence, (ahimsa), authenticity/veracity (satya), not stealing (asteya), austerity (aparigraha) and chastity (brahmacharya). As Xavier Melloni points out in his book, *El Uno en lo multiple* (The

One in the Multiple), we can see the parallels between these five yama and the Hebrew Decalogue: non-violence (ahimsa) picks up on and widens the commandment not to kill; veracity picks up on and widens the precept of not lying; austerity can be placed in relation to not being envious, and chastity with the sixth and ninth commandments.

The Buddhists also propose various basic principles: do not kill any live being, do not steal, do not have illicit sexual relationships, do not lie and do not drink alcoholic drinks.

Xavier Melloni summarises thus the Four Noble Truths that Buddha reached after his enlightenment:

1. Existence is full of pain.
2. This suffering comes from the avidness of desire, which has these areas: foods, the senses, the desires of the will and of consciousness.
3. The method with which to free oneself from these desires is detachment and letting go, which is achieved on stopping the identification with the ego, which is what feels attraction or rejection for people and things.
4. The letting go, followed by the enlightenment that it brings, is achieved through the eight attitudes: the correct vision, the correct understanding, the correct speaking, the correct action, the correct way of life, the correct effort, the correct attention and the correct concentration.

The correct speaking implies not lying, not speaking badly of others, not causing rumours or exaggerating; the correct action consists of not harming others, not killing or stealing, and offering help for them to find the path of realisation; and the correct way of life consists of living with honour and avoiding all kind of unjust behaviour.

In the Bhagavad-Gita, idolatry is associated with the self-centred desire: "Those whose intelligence has been stolen by material desires surrender unto semi gods and, guided by their inferior nature, they get lost along many other paths." (BG 7, 20). "Desire darkens everything." (BG 3, 38). "Attachment arises out of satisfying the pleasures of the senses; from attachment arises desire, lust and the anxiety to possess; and that leads to anger." (BG 2, 62). (Another translation of BG 2, 62 is: While contemplating the objects of the senses, a person develops attachment for them, and from such attachment lust develops, and from lust anger arises.) On the contrary, "true peace can only be found by the person who has given up all the desires to please the senses, who lives free from desires, who has given up on all sense of possession (proprietorship) and who is stripped of false ego." (BG 2, 71).

Thus, we see how religions offer a moral code in order to point out the limits of the ego and help us to transcend it. They are guidelines for behaviour that differ little in the fundamental axes. They all turn in relation to the control over one's own compulsive desires. However, these moral codes or disciplines mark some guidelines, but they do not show us how to manage to put them into practice successfully.

The different spiritual paths that arise within and outside of religions, offer the necessary instruments in order to walk on the path integrating the dimensions of the self in practical life. Walking on the path, the pilgrim, the traveller, finally manages to strengthen his heart, reaching a greater generosity by transcending the small self, because he has become pure love – total love. This process implies various deaths, given that the ego is like an onion that has many layers, and we remove them to the extent that we allow them to die. It is a process of 'dying in life', because you continue here, alive, conscious, but a part of you, of your ego, dissolves along the way in the measure that you advance towards self-realisation and towards the awareness of union.

To get out of the state of ignorance, where the ego predominates, all the spiritual paths propose the regular practice of prayer or meditation, where one realises that to empty oneself and dissolve the ego, is not to annihilate the self, but rather the possibility of a greater communion that elevates being to a wider and more universal awareness.

Some devote themselves completely to meditation with the intention of elevating their awareness. But this is not possible unless one remains seated, rooted and present in the now. Some make the mistake of isolating themselves from the world, of separating themselves from the world and shared life, devoting their time and energy to mystical and meditative practices with the intention of transcending it all. Then they wonder why their progress is slow.

The real lessons that have to be learned and integrated, in order to then transcend, take place in shared places, in the day to day, with daily interactions with people and with the practical aspects of daily life. When people, places and practical aspects are not treated with love and care, they become a burden that we carry within as pending matters. This burden pushes us down and prevents us from transcending.

As well as meditation it is also proposed that one involves oneself in some kind of humble service that frees us from the need of others' appreciation; in doing so, we are not to expect personal benefits from our actions; placing oneself at the disposition of a person or of others in general. This is called karma yoga; actions of service to the other that helps someone to let go of their ego.

In all religious traditions, life in community is also proposed, given that this facilitates and accelerates the process of letting go of one's own selfish self in order to enter into communion with others and with God.

From this perspective, freedom is not understood as doing what I want, when I want and how I want, but it is rather a freedom that implies freeing oneself from the limited self, the selfish, greedy, violent, attached and ignorant self in order to reveal the authentic self – the true being which is love, is peace, is aware, knowing and free. In this state you enjoy solitude, because it is not a solitude in which you are running away or isolating yourself from the world. You also enjoy shared living because you do not allow the other to wound you or to dominate you. That way you live in freedom being alone and living together.

The Power of Circumstances

There are periods of life in which it seems to us that there is someone or something who gets in the way of our path. Circumstances, instead of going in our favour, go against us. They are barriers that make it difficult for us to reach our objectives; they are interruptions that prevent us from feeling satisfied; they are situations that seem to sabotage our efficiency.

When we find ourselves with these scenes that appear to impede our progress towards the objectives that we have set out for ourselves, we tend to have negative thoughts; we feel anger and rage, or we feel sad and lacking in spirit, as if we don't have the strength to either overcome or transform the situation. Rather it is the situation that overcomes us and leaves us exhausted.

Some people are not prepared for this to happen and put all their strength into fighting against it. They do so from anger and the feeling of injustice. Often it becomes a process that wastes their energies and leaves them exhausted, without achieving a true advancement. It is not a good methodology to act by forcing something with anger.

It is possible to live through situations without them causing us such an emotional cost. That does not mean that we become cold and insensitive in the face of what happens around us. It is a question of living through situations without collapsing into them. If we drown ourselves in them we won't be able to help anybody, or ourselves. We will be lost, like the shipwrecked, at the mercy of the waves, the tides and the winds. We will have lost the control of the steering wheel of our ship – our life.

The challenge lies in knowing what the strategy is to learn to live through situations without allowing them to determine our emotional and mental state. It is a matter of living without circumstances being the creators of such unhappiness, stress, suffering, sadness, frustration and anger in our lives.

In order to achieve it, in the first place, we should change our interpretation. Instead of interpreting the fact as an obstruction, interference or barrier to our path, we might change our perception. It can help us to ask questions like: What has this situation taught me? What does it say to me? Observe and listen before reacting immediately. From observation and listening we can have a more objective and wider perception. Nothing happens by chance.

We are the creators of our realities. Reality, in itself, does not create for us stress, pain or unhappiness. It is our perception and interpretation of reality that brings about these reactions. Therefore, we have to review how we perceive situations and with what beliefs we interpret and judge them.

Reinterpreting the situation, the concrete reality, implies allowing the old perception to die in order to make room for a new vision. Without the old dying, the new cannot be built correctly.

Instead of seeing people or situations as obstacles on the path, we can see them as opportunities to practise patience and tolerance, to know how to listen, thank and love. They give us the opportunity to detach ourselves and to take a healthy distance in order to look with objectivity. They help us to set out again to ourselves our objectives. They allow us to widen our capacity to co-operate and enlarge our heart so that we might be more generous.

In order to have a wider perception and not to drown in the situation, you can position yourself in another way. If you stabilise yourself in respect towards yourself, in maintaining your self-esteem and a healthy distance (not necessarily physical, but rather by not letting the situation absorb you), you will be able to have an eagle's vision. From above, everything looks smaller. It is easier to get over something small. You can.

Whatever happens, it is important to always be aware that you create your thoughts and you allow the images to have greater or lesser impact inside you, according to how you interiorise them. Learn to create thoughts full of love, courage, trust and determination. Those thoughts, charged with positive energy, will help you to allow each situation to pass; to really overcome it and leave it behind; for it not to remain alive in your thoughts or in your memory.

With the power of a mind that creates thoughts full of good energy, wherever you go, you will create a pleasant atmosphere. Your vibrations will give off and create spaces and situations full of beauty, trust and tranquillity; spaces where all those who enter will remove their masks and will connect again with the authenticity of their being.

Free Yourself of Pressures

When we feel pressured, it seems that other forces rule our life and we do not feel free. Can we only live in freedom when there is an absence of outside pressure? We feel pressured from many sides. At work, we feel the pressure to fulfil a timetable and deadlines. In relationships, we feel the pressure to satisfy and fulfil the expectations that the other has placed in us. In studies, we feel the pressure of the exam dates. In exams, we feel the pressure of having to pass. In the face of a problem, we feel pressure when there are circumstances that seem to prevent us from solving it quickly or in the way that we want. And so life turns into an endless amount of pressure points that appear, one after the other, without giving us time to breathe.

Is it necessary to feel pressured? Frankly, it is unnecessary. When we believe that something 'bad' or negative can happen if we don't reach the objective or the achievement that we set ourselves or that others set us, we feel pressured. The fear of failure generates pressure in us. The fear of being abandoned pressurises us to fulfil the expectations of others.

Sometimes, we put pressure on ourselves, believing that a bit of pressure is good in order to achieve what we want; it provides us with adrenaline and energy. In the long-term, this repetitive habit of creating feelings of pressure ends up by leaving us exhausted.

Working under pressure reduces our skills of thinking clearly, discerning well and acting correctly. Until you realise, you don't decide to change the habit.

While you blame situations, the expectations of others, and the deadlines they place on you as the causes of your stress and pressure, you will be able to do little to change the habit.

It is you that pressurises yourself and allows the outside to pressurise you. You can either come to fulfil your objective with anxiety, pressure, stress and a feeling of being trapped and hurried, or you can fulfil it with trust, determination, giving of yourself, perseverance, maintaining tranquillity and emotional stability. How you experience it depends on you.

To relieve the pressure, ask yourself: why do you feel pressured? Observe the feeling. Where does it come from? What are you afraid of? Don't allow the fear to invade you by exercising pressure, anxiety and panic.

Stopping and observing will help you to put a brake on the feeling that you are creating. Discover what thoughts are behind the feeling of pressure that you feel. "Perhaps I won't arrive on time." "If I don't hand it in on time, I will lose the work." "If I don't do this, they will stop appreciating me." In these kinds of thoughts there is the fear of losing something if you do not manage to satisfy some expectations. This fear exercises a pressure that reduces your capacity to achieve your objectives.

For this not to happen, you should change the course of thoughts that you are having. Have thoughts of trust and enthu-siasm instead of thoughts burdened with insecurity and fears. To do so you have to realise what the beliefs are that influence you in the creation of your thoughts. There are thoughts that are determined by your belief of what success is and what failure is, what winning is and what losing is. There are beliefs that, although we believe them, are not true; they are like a veil that prevent us from seeing clearly and generate in us feelings of fear and feelings of pressure.

Stopping yourself, observing, reinterpreting, re-evaluating, controlling thoughts and feelings and changing beliefs requires energy. Not an energy that we will obtain from the outside, but rather the energy of truth that we carry within. The power of truth, of authenticity, provides us with the necessary energy to change. The truth is deeper than beliefs. In fact, many beliefs are false and that is why they bring about in us states of anxiety and suffering when we allow them to influence our perception of reality.

Let us look at some examples of how to disconnect from the habit of creating pressure and connecting to the power of truth:

The Pressure of Deadlines
The belief that causes pressure is that if the work isn't done in the given time, something bad will happen.

The truth that relieves the pressure is that nobody loses anything if, for once, they don't manage to hand in the work on time or even, if they were to lose the job, they would be able to find another one. Their health is the most important thing. If they lose the job, they can find another one, but, if due to the pressure of work, they lose their health, it is more difficult to get it back.

Pressure on the Level of Achievement
The belief that causes pressure is that perhaps I will not reach the level of achievement that I have set out for myself; perhaps I will not reach the standard that I have imposed on myself.

The truth that relieves the pressure is that I can only do the best of my capacity at that moment. If I don't reach the level I have set out for myself this time, I will strengthen myself and learn in this attempt to improve the next.

Pressure Due to Economic Commitments

The belief that causes pressure is that perhaps I will not be able to get all the money that I need in order to meet my commitments.

The truth that relieves the pressure is that I can only pay with the money I have, and, if there isn't enough, I will simple have to reduce my commitments.

Pressure about the Future

The belief that causes pressure is that for sure things are going to get worse the next week, the coming months, next year.

The truth that relieves the pressure is that everything always changes. There are always reasons for the changes that take place, and really nothing gets worse; it is simple different.

Pressure because of Others' Expectations

The belief that causes pressure is that I have to satisfy the expectations of others or, if not, I will lose their approval and that will affect my self-esteem.

The truth that relieves the pressure is that I do not 'have to' fulfil anyone's expectations, although I can choose to do so, and I do not depend on the approval of others to keep my self-esteem.

Pressure Due to Health Matters

The belief that causes pressure is that my health seems to get worse and worse.

The truth that relieves the pressure is that all physical pain is caused by a weakness, something bad, is leaving the body; it is dissolving and being healed. Therefore, it is good. All mental and emotional suffering is a messenger that says that I should change something on the level of thoughts and feelings.

Pressure Due to Objectives and Ambitions

The belief that causes pressure is that I have to reach my goals in order to be happy and successful.

The truth that relieves the pressure is that I can be happy without needing to achieve my goals, and only when I am happy does it make sense to reach for any goal, and I do so easily.

All feelings of pressure have in common the belief that, perhaps, you lose something if... And the truth that relieves the pressure in each case is that you have nothing to lose, given that, in reality, nothing is yours.

Note: Some of the ideas of this section have been taken from the weekly writings *Clear Thinking*, by Mike George. www.relax7.com

Living at Peace with Time

To live in freedom you have to live at peace with time; live the dimension of time as a creator of time and not a slave of time; live without being either a prisoner or victim of time.

To live at peace with time is to live in harmony with nature, beginning with your inner nature. When you plant a seed today, you cannot accelerate the process so that the next day you have a fruit tree. When it is night, you cannot make the earth move quicker or slower for the sun to come out before or later. Everything has its rhythm in nature.

We have distanced ourselves from the natural rhythm and our accelerated mind exercises pressure, creates stress and causes anxiety. We plan the future, we are stuck in the past and the present escapes us.

Many worries have to do with how we live time: the past, the present and the future. Worrying about what might happen, when the moment has not yet come for it to happen, takes away from us the necessary energy to deal with it when it finally arrives.

Living in memories drains our energy; the past already happened and no longer exists, except in our memory. We feed memories, not realising that living off the memory distracts us from the present and weakens us. It is like being a plug that connects to a socket with no current passing through. We lose our energy. We want to relive an experience that already happened, and in the end we feel disappointed, feeling a mental and emotional waste.

Not only is your strength reduced by the way that you live the past and project onto the future, but also how you live in this moment. When, for example, you oppose the present and have resistances, these consume your energy and cause you stress. If you accept the present you can flow flexibly without wasting your energy. Accepting does not mean submitting yourself or feeling a victim of what is happening now. From acceptance, you confront and transform.

If we learn to live the dimensions of time in a healthy way we will keep up our vitality, we will heal the past and we will feel at peace with it. Accepting the present and trusting in the future helps us to be well.

Accepting the present means stopping comparing yourself with others; you want what the other has, their properties, their talents, their beauty and their achievements. So, instead of being grateful for what you have and accepting yourself as you are, you try to have and be like the other. In this way, you are never satisfied. The dissatisfaction causes you a constant unhappiness that reduces your vitality. When you feel happy and satisfied your energy flows more easily.

The most important thing that you should do in this moment is to feel fine. Next, what is the most important thing? To be fine. Therefore, the priority, and what is essential, is that whatever happens in the moment, the most important thing is to be fine. So, tell your mind, "Oh, mind, be quiet and don't think so much. Oh, mind, trust." Give your mind the basic instructions and the key thoughts with which to be fine. Don't let your own mind create the thoughts that trap you. It is we ourselves who create our cage.

To live at peace with time is to live it with serenity, trust and determination. It is different to living it out of conflict and forcing things. In order to live true freedom of being, we have to make friends with time and stop living stressed in time. We have to trust. Trust that you will arrive on time, that you will do it on time and, if not, that it will be solved. Don't let time be a stress factor.

When we live stressed because of time, we lose the best of life. We stop living what is essential and important, and we get lost in the details: I have to go here, I have to do this, I have to ring someone, and an endless amounts of 'I have tos' that consume our mental energy and make us get lost in the details of the trivial. As well, in hurrying, we lose quality. You can do everything, but without losing what is essential; do it with love, with care, with interest, with enthusiasm, with motivation. That way that small action that you take will have a greater impact.

You choose whether, each morning, you want to get up and begin with the radio, smoking and a coffee, or you want to get up and meditate, listen to peaceful music, read something that inspires you and begin the day visualising it positively: today will be a marvellous day.

Personally, at the beginning of the day, early in the morning, at daybreak, I begin with a mediation. Meditation connects me with the eternity of time. It seems as if time were elastic, in such a way that a minute can seem eternal or can seem an instant. Thus, I learn to be a creator of time; living in time without being enslaved by it.

True freedom lies in being fine now. You can be fine in the present moment by resolving the inner dialogue that generates stress and conflict in you. When you are fine, enjoying yourself and having a good time, you don't realise how time passes. This means that, if we lived in a state of constant happiness, we wouldn't realise how time passes. Time would be at our service.

You Choose How You Respond

Embracing Change
We are living through situations of constant change. Even now,

while you read this book, perhaps it seems to you that you are still, but it is not so. The earth turns on itself and around the sun. Although the chair, the armchair or the bed seem to be still, they are moving through the space of the Universe; kept in one place which appears fixed by the force of gravity. The cells of your body are regenerating themselves, some dying and some being born. The air that you breathe goes in and out and moves through space. The energy of your thought and your being are also changing.

In fact, we cannot cling on to anything because what is now will not be, and what was is already not. The idea that something is ours and that we possess it is, to a certain extent, false, given that we cannot hang onto anything, since everything is in constant change. In the highest and most authentic reality we possess nothing. Everything comes and it goes. Nothing remains as it was. It changes shape, colour, composition, position or place. When we become aware of this reality, we enter into a space of inner freedom in which we know that, on not being able to hold onto anything, all pressures and stress terminate. Before we were occupied in maintaining attachments, clinging hard onto them and, therefore, we were less open to receiving. Now, with this change in perception and living out of a more authentic reality, we are more available and more open to receiving and embracing change.

In the face of change we can respond in many ways: clinging onto what it was before the change, adapting to what comes, resisting, rejecting it, fleeing, ignoring what is happening, avoiding it, embracing it, strengthening it...

You choose your response. There are responses that tie you, they upset you, they exhaust you, they weaken you, they annul you or they depress you. There are answers that strengthen you. They are answers that help you to give the most of yourself, widen your generosity, your capacity for understanding and your tolerance. There are responses that isolate you. Others communicate you with the other and with the world.

And the good news is that you choose what you are going to do. You have the possibility and the freedom to use your creative capacity in order to respond to the reality that surrounds you and the stimuli that it throws at you every moment. This means to change the predominant belief that the other – others, society or the world – determine how you are and why you react as you do.

If you justify your responses by blaming the outside, you diminish your power to choose the response. For example, if you say that you are sad each time that it rains, then your sadness depends on whether it rains or not; therefore, you are giving up on your freedom to choose whether you get sad or not because you depend on the weather. Let's see an example: the plumber has to come to fix a leak. He should have come at ten in the morning, but it is one o'clock and he still hasn't come. The day ends and he still hasn't come. You ring him and he doesn't answer, so you spend the day stressed out because the plumber doesn't come. You can choose to respond differently, find another solution. But while he doesn't come, how many useless thoughts do you have? How many negative thoughts? How upset do you get? How stressed do you get? How worried do you get? All these thoughts and feelings you create yourself. That is your freedom of creation. Perhaps the plumber has had an accident, perhaps his previous job got complicated, whatever... Is he in control of your life in those moments?

We end up by being the victims of everything that happens around us and of all those who intervene in our life, because we consider that everything and everyone is guilty of how we respond. We give up our power to choose to external circumstances and then we become the victims of them.

We don't accept things as they come to us, situations as they happen to us or others as they act with us. We would like it to be different and we resist accepting it. Resisting takes up a lot of energy and it weakens us. Accepting does not mean being in agreement. It is keeping your energy concentrated in order to create the right response that will take you towards the results that you want. The important thing is to be fine.

When an important change takes place in your life, observe your response. If you resist accepting the change it is because you are afraid; afraid of losing something. Perhaps you might lose your position, a property, possession or money. The change might mean that you lose privileges or prestige. Perhaps with the change you lose the closeness of a person or a place.

In life, all these things – summarised as the seven Ps (position, property, pay, privileges, prestige, person or place) – come and go and then others appear, which will also go. It is like a river in constant movement. If we try to stop the flow of the river, we create a dam; the water stagnates and causes a pressure which accumulates inside us.

To learn to let go, to not cling and allow the flow, is to live without resistances; being the creators of constructive changes that bring about improvements and widen our horizons. In order to have this capacity of creative and positive response, it is necessary to balance action with going into oneself, silence, reflection and meditation. We attain the capacity to live in harmony when our action is balanced with reflection and strengthened by silence.

In the silence we get our strength back, we clarify ideas and we learn to trust in our intuition. Then we act out of the heart of our being. Our responses arise out of love and trust and not out of fear or bitterness.

Remember that between thought and action there is a space. In that space, which can be a thousandth of a second, various seconds or a few minutes, you can change the direction of your thoughts and choose your action, so that it is not an impulsive reaction influenced by your negative energies or those of your surroundings. Meditation helps you to create the habit of responding out of serenity and in an aware way.

In a piece of research that was carried out some years ago in the prisons of India, they asked the inmates, that had killed, if they had stopped to think for five minutes before committing the crime, would they still have done it? 85% said that they wouldn't; they acted out of impulse, without reflecting and without being able to control their reaction. If they had stopped for a few minutes they would have calmed down, or at least they would have been able to control their anger and they wouldn't have killed.

A reaction can change the direction of your life and that of many people. Reflect. Meditate. Learn to respond out of serenity, with clarity and determination, with patience and humility, with love and self-giving and with a sense of humour. Learn to play with the waves that come and go, like the surfer.

Say YES or Say NO

In life we are presented with situations that seem to ask something of us or offer us opportunities. They make us question what we are doing and suggest to us that perhaps we should change direction.

To embrace life is to embrace the change that situations suggest to us, as long as it is in agreement with our conscience and our heart. A recent example is that of Jaume Sanllorente, who went to India as a tourist and ended up creating the NGO Smiles of Bombay, www.bombaysmiles.org. He had his life well set up in Barcelona, but upon seeing an orphanage in Bombay, on the point of closing its doors because of lack of funds, he felt a calling and said YES to this calling. Although many tried to convince him that he should say NO, he listened to his heart.

We are capable of bringing changes to humanity and to our world, and can create platforms where an improvement is possible. We should be clear about what we say YES to, and what we say NO to.

When you put your heart into something and your mind

centres itself, the energy flows powerfully towards there. It is a question of listening to your heart, and daring to say YES and to say NO. We have to say it keeping our conscience and action in line, in order to maintain integrity and coherence.

Personally, I have lived through difficult and uncomfortable situations, but in my heart I knew that I had to be there. The trust in myself, and the confidence that everything would work out fine, knowing that there was some hidden lesson that I had to learn, helped me to say YES. It was what the moment and the situation asked of me, although I would have preferred to be in some other 'more comfortable' place – a less risky one. It was important to hear the voice of time, the voice of the moment, the voice of the situation and trust that it would strengthen me, with which it would bring me closer to a greater personal development and to my destiny as a person, who makes up a part of humanity. That is, it was a personal benefit and a global benefit. On strengthening myself and widening my limits I would be able and/or share better with others.

When you are faced with different situations, proposals and opportunities, which do you say YES to and which do you say NO to?

In order to decide, it is important to keep the vision of your dream, your longings, what your soul really wants, in front of you. Be aware of what is essential for you. From this space of inner clarity, we should see which of these situations/opportunities follow the direction of your dream, what is essential and what distances you; they are like 'mirages' that seem to offer something easy and attractive, but which distance you from the essential. They are opportunities that seem easier and, out of laziness, it would be easier to say YES. But within you, if you listen, you know that, in the long or short term, you will not be happy, given that you have avoided or are running away from the challenge, you haven't listened to your heart. You have allowed yourself to be lead by inertia. Gandhi wrote "We should refuse to allow ourselves to be carried by the current. A human being who is drowning cannot save others."

When you say YES to the project, situation or action that is close to your ideal, it is a YES in which there is not submission, where you do not lose your freedom or your light. It is a YES with the certainty that, learning from what life offers you, you leap forward and get close to universal wisdom, where you feel love in freedom and acceptance without resentment or resignation.

Personally, in order to say YES with enthusiasm and openness, embracing what was coming without knowing very well what to expect, I have had to work with myself on acceptance, disappointments, broken dreams and ruptures.

Sometimes the rupture is not so much with something external, but rather something that breaks inside you. You question how you have been living until now, and your beliefs begin to seem limited to you. You feel uncertainty and perhaps you want to cry; what you used to lean on can no longer continue to be a pillar for you and you find yourself in a void and alone. You know that you have to let go but you don't know where to hang on to.

Firstly, you don't have to be alarmed – it is a good sign that this rupture takes place inside you! Don't be afraid! Remember that life is energy in constant change, and nothing remains fixed; we live birth and death various times inside us. You have to be prepared to be reborn and to allow what is no use any more to die.

Value what has been of use to you until now, and when you don't need it any more, have the capacity to let go, allow it to go; that way, creating space to embrace the new. You feel that it is a challenge because it seems that you have to jump into the void, given that you don't know what really awaits you and cannot find the place on which to lean. Your beliefs and your habits seem limited and you need to breathe new air that helps you in the new stage that you are beginning.

It is the opportunity to revise your dreams. What is it that your soul really longs to reach? Remember that your creative capacity is extraordinary; trust in yourself and cultivate your inner resources in order to achieve your aims.

Creativity, flexibility and trust are the key to living through this rupture with the old – the past – and accepting the new – the unknown and uncertain. Creativity is necessary for you to visualise and realise your purpose; getting closer to your idea in a new form.

Flexibility is essential to adapt to changes and is it critical to trust that all will go well; you will know other facets of yourself; you will become aware of the great potential that you have that is yet to awaken, and you will find new helps, new friendships; other opportunities will appear and you will glimpse new horizons that will regenerate your enthusiasm and motivation. This will strengthen your self-esteem. Self-esteem is the base from which to stop saying YES in the situations when we know we should say NO. Being brave in order to say NO implies that you dare to lose the possible approval of the other. How many times do we say YES in order to receive the approval of the other?

Although we know in our conscience that we should say NO, we say YES out of the fear of offending, out of the fear of seeming incapable, shame, to avoid a confrontation or even out of the guilt of not being there for someone. Then it is a YES with submission.

Whether we say YES or NO, when the decision is based on some fear, we will have to justify it, defend it, and, internally, we will feel insecure because our heart is not there. A decision based on fear and with the objective of maintaining an apparent security, paradoxically, keeps us insecure within.

It is a matter of learning to say YES or to say NO with assertiveness, with respect towards oneself and the other and with self-esteem. That way you won't need to justify or defend your decisions. If you have to justify your NO, it means that there is some hole in your self-esteem and, through this hole, influences will enter that will manipulate you or rule over your decisions.

To say NO with assertiveness and with positive energy implies that you have reflected upon it and that you have good reasons to say NO, which do not go against anyone or anything. That is, your NO arises out of a positive energy and not out of rejection or bitterness. You recognise that there is something to do, you feel empathy towards the person or situation and you value it. But you explain to the other person that now, for you, it is not the moment. With empathy, you achieve the agreement of the other person; you offer alternatives, solutions or creative ideas, showing your care and attention. In this sense, the NO is a positive NO, which arises out of a space of love, courage and respect. It is to say YES to say NO.

The word YES has an affirmative power. Good thoughts and actions have a universally positive impact. We have created the space, Yesouisi, which starts with the power of the YES. Yes – Oui – Sí: YES in English, French and Spanish (Si is also Italian and Portuguese). Yesouisi, in its English pronunciation, would be: Yes we see. It gives us the meaning of awakening and seeing, becoming aware and realising all of our potential. You can visit the website – www.yesouisi.es

Your Inner World: Personal Power

In the previous chapters we have seen that, if internally we are not strong, stable and do not have control over our mind or emotional world, the outside controls us; it causes us to fluctuate, and ends up by weakening us and bringing us down. However, our inner flame does not extinguish.

Thanks to the inner strength that lies hidden in each one of us, we survive adversity and difficult circumstances. In times of crisis, depression and disappointment, this inner strength helps us to recover. Our capacity to overcome critical or catastrophic situations is extraordinary. We have a great potential that seems to awaken in these circumstances.

The question is what happens to this capacity when things go more or less well, in the day to day. For what, when and where do we use the potential that we carry within? Does it only awaken when we face difficulties? It seems that, when we are in the 'normality' of the day to day, we fall into a lack of care and laziness; we lose our mental clarity and we are weakened. Then we complain, we criticise and we lament. Our capacity to live in wholeness and not to be conquered by the influences that weaken us atrophy.

When situations control you and enter into your being, you no longer control the ship of your life, you lose direction and you go down. Your thoughts weaken and your feelings are of being trapped and stifled. Your mind shoots off and you don't stop worrying. You get distracted and your vital strength is dissipated. You lose attention and your energy is dispersed.

In one of their weekly visits to the master, the disciple left, as was the custom, his sandals outside the door, and went in barefoot in order to meet him again. On that occasion the master asked him where he had left the sandals: on the right or the left of the door. The disciple, surprised, answered him that he had not realised. The master told him that that was a sign that he hadn't focused the meditation well, given that good meditation helps you to be attentive. He explained to him that if we don't pay attention to each action, if we allow the mind to wander while we are acting, and then don't know where we have put the handkerchief, the keys, or, in this case, the sandals, inner power disperses and we waste time looking for things; we waste time and clarity because we have not been attentive.

Sometimes you think 'I am going to do this', then another thought comes, and another, and another one... Some hours pass before you realise: "Ah, I was going to do that and I haven't done it!" The thought came to you but why didn't you do it? You had many thoughts, one after another, and you didn't have concentration, clarity or focus. Then you go from one task to another and leave things half-done, unfinished. Your list of what is pending becomes interminable and the disorder, lack of organisation and care increase in your life. What is more, if you do something without being sure of what you want to do, doubting and afraid of failing, whatever you do will not have strength.

Let us look at some factors that help us to recover our personal power.

Aligning Awareness, Decision and Action

If your mind thinks too fast and one thought runs over another, your intellect doubts and cannot decide, your past conditions you and traps you, and your habits lead you to worry without cease; no doubt your ship will sink once and again in the circumstances that surround you.

To avoid this happening to you, you have to recover your inner power, be alert and pay attention. That way you do not allow situations to absorb you and, slowly, destroy your calm, sinking you into a river of preoccupations. You need to have a greater control of your inner world: of your mind, intellect, tendencies, conditionings and habits.

On the one hand, it is a matter of controlling your thoughts, having clarity in your decisions and not allowing your unhealthy habits to control you. On the other hand, your inner power lies in not thinking one thing, feeling another, saying another and finally acting differently. You have to listen to your conscience, given that it is the steering wheel of your life. If you listen to it, your decisions will be based on what your integrity and strength maintain. That way, in your actions, you will manage to express all your potential by helping yourself and others. When you act with a clear vision, with self-esteem, trust and serenity, you have the capacity to carry out your aims successfully. On doing it thus, you will feel satisfied.

When, on the contrary, what you do is not what you think or what you say, your words lose strength. When a father says to his son not to do something, but he does it, these words do not have strength, given that they do not have the power of the example. The son listens to the advice of the father but he sees that he does not follow it. This sows a doubt in him: "Why does he advise me this but not do it himself?"

On one occasion, when the participants were preparing to take part in the round table on threats to environmental pollution and possible solutions in Sao Paulo, the Environment Minister was smoking in such a way that he resembled a walking chimney; one cigarette after another. On the one hand, he spoke to propose solutions to pollution, and on the other, he lived like a chimney on legs. This lack of integrity between what one thinks, says and does, brings about a loss of power in action, a lack of coherence and a diminishing of trust.

What happens is that at times your conscience requires you to go in one direction but your acquired habits lead you in another very different one. Then, who rules? The conscience that is nourished by your values, or your habits? At that moment you have to ask yourself: what do I really want? Listen to the voice of your heart, of the centre of your being. That way you will connect to your inner wisdom and your innate strength, which will help you to overcome the habit.

We have already seen that you choose how you respond in the face of the stimuli that others and circumstances create around you. Recognise that you are responsible for your thoughts, words and actions. This is the initial base in order to get back your inner power. As Osho reminds in his book, *Satyam, Shivam, Sundaram: Truth, Godliness and Beauty*, "Responsibility is one side of the coin and the other is freedom. You can have the two things together, or abandon them together. If you don't want responsibility, neither will you have freedom, and without freedom there is no growth. You can lead a happy life, but there are not two paths, only one: being yourself, being what you are"

"The greatest victory is the one that you win over yourself," Buddha told us.

Live in harmony with what you think, what you say and what you do. To do so, you have to be permanently in contact with your inner strengths, your capacity to see, to realise, to discern, choose and decide. On having full government of your decisions, you will feel free. Without this mastery, you are not free. Living in freedom, you feel your strength and vital energy fully.

Being free is like playing the piano. If you have a piano and hands to play it, do you feel free to do so? You need skills; to strengthen your fingers so that your arms and shoulders do not tense up; to know the instrument in order to control it; to understand the language of music; to refine your hearing and tune the piano, to study and practise with discipline. That way you will be able to play and to enjoy it. Living in freedom also requires mastery, strengthening, understanding and discipline.

Each situation in life is an opportunity to practise and exercise our freedom. To free oneself of guilt, of complaints, of excuses and of anger is vital in order to exercise our freedom. Evidently, we are free to blame, to complain, make excuses and feel anger for all the injustices that we see and suffer from. However, at the moment that we use our freedom to blame, lament, make excuses and feel anger, we lose our mastery over situations. Our energy and our mental clarity are reduced; our happiness goes and we end up being victims of what is around us.

Do we want to be the creator of a new reality where what rules is love, honesty, respect and hope?

In order to be the creators of the change that this implies and build a better reality, we have to do it out of authenticity, love, courage and inner power. The other attitudes (complaining, anger and blame) weaken us and prolong the creation of atmospheres and situations of stress and violence.

In all areas of life, we have the freedom to use our immense creative power. To do so is in our hands.

Let us see how to overcome these attitudes that weaken us.

Complaints: Is Everything Fine? Nothing is Going Well

We live in a world full of imperfections, and, luckily, we are not perfect either. I say luckily because being imperfect offers us the possibilities of learning, change and hope. It stimulates us to make an effort and it prevents us from getting bored. The theme of perfection and imperfection, what is and isn't perfect, I will leave for another book! There is so much to learn and do in this imperfect world! Learning to go from doing towards being is, in itself, a great work, whereby the achievement lies in inverting the terms: going from being to doing, acting from the self. However, for the one who complains it seems that the world ought to be perfect. With such a habit it becomes something natural to think how things should or shouldn't be or could or could not be.

When you complain, your energy and clarity diminish and your unhappiness increases. You don't accept what there is or what is, as it is. Your complaints lead you to criticism and to useless gossip. In these kinds of conversations time and energy are lost and mistrust and unhappiness are generated. Relationships are harmed and then require a good investment of time and energy to get back the lost trust.

Someone who complains regularly, and is compulsively angry, expects the world to make them happy and the Universe to dance to their music. As things are almost never as they want, they are in a state of constant complaint. They don't realise that happiness comes from within and is cultivated within. They expect situations and others to make them happy. And, as this does not come to pass, they complain constantly.

The person who often complains despairs and gets discouraged. They feel that they cannot do anything to change what they would like to change. They feel impotent.

The person who almost never complains has realised that every time they complain they focus on something negative, and the first person to suffer is, in effect, themselves, since it diminishes their energy level and they feel worse.

The person who never complains accepts what is as it is, what comes as it comes, and what happens as it happens. However, if they consider that something has to be changed, they put their energy into making it happen.

Mike George, in one of his weekly reflections (*Clear Thinking*, number 78, September 2007), gives us a clear example of the reaction of a compulsive complainer and of someone who never complains in the face of the same situation: both have met for dinner. On realising that they have little to say to each other, they decide to sit on separate tables. When the starter arrives, the soup, it arrives cold on both tables. The complainer suffers and reacts immediately by making a great complaint to the waiter. He gets into such a bad mood because of the cold soup that it generates a really unhappy feeling in him. The waiter, of course, gets a bit defensive. The one that doesn't complain does not remain quiet and eat the soup. He calls the waiter and informs him that the soup is cold and asks for it to be warmed. He doesn't get angry or into a bad mood; therefore, he doesn't suffer. He accepts that, at times, the Universe serves the soup a bit cold! To inform and ask is not to complain; it is to give feedback and to make a request. The difference between both is the difference between an emotional reaction and a proactive response.

If there is something that doesn't go as you would like it to go, use mental energy to construct, create, transform or solve.

Excuses: The Mind Deceives You

When you are not sure whether you want something or not, or when your heart pushes you towards something but your reasoning prevents it, then, as you struggle to decide, any pretext is good to turn into an excuse. You want to go on a trip, but you are afraid. As you are ashamed to recognise that fear paralyses you, you somatise the situation and you become ill. You can't go on a trip because you are ill. And you believe it. You don't recognise that you have somatised your conflict of whether to go or not go, and, as you couldn't decide, finally the illness decides. Or you want to see someone and clear some things up, but your fears and insecurities make you put off the appointment. You want to but you don't want to. Sometimes you know it is good for you to do something but you resist it. Then you say that now you can't.

A lady called Sonia used to come to meditate at the meditation centre. She wanted to devote herself to it more, but she said that she couldn't because of her husband. She really wanted to, but he stopped her. After her husband died, I thought that she would participate more in the activities of the meditation centre, since that was her desire. However, she had a dog and she had to take care of it to such a point that it kept her tied to the house and to the dog. When the dog died, I thought, 'Now Sonia is free and will be more participative in order to carry out her dreams.' But her son had twins and the mother didn't look after them very well. So Sonia became a grandmother who was needed morning, afternoon and night by her grandchildren.

So the reality is that neither the husband nor the dog or grandchildren could prevent Sonia from expressing all her potential and achieving her dreams. She used them as an excuse because, on the one hand, she wasn't clear about it, and on the other, she was afraid of letting go and in the end she preferred to remain asleep in the face of creating her own destiny. That way, she did not take on 100% the responsibility for her life and was able to use others as excuses not to hear the voice of her conscience. Sonia could have carried out all her responsibilities and, at the same time, exercised her freedom to participate in the creative activities that she might want to. Perhaps she was afraid of losing others' approval. Perhaps the charge of 'not being a good wife', not being a 'good grandmother', prevented her from being who she wanted to be and doing what she wanted to do.

We cannot judge what others do or why they take the decisions that they take. Every person has their reasons. The important thing is that one does not deceive him/herself.

The mind is so strong that it keeps us asleep, unaware, creating excuses that we believe are true.

If you want something but you don't want it, be sincere with yourself. Don't use the world as an excuse to not achieve or do want you want; in doing so, you deceive yourself; you endanger your health, distance yourself from your happiness and you lose your freedom. You live in a contradiction between what you want and what you really do. In order to deny that the problem is in you, you make excuses not to act, not to achieve, not to be and not express what you would like in your heart. Stop deceiving yourself and everything will go better. Try it. Don't be afraid.

Don't let your body suffer the somatisation of your contradictions, and if it happens, if your body somatises, LISTEN.

The world needs people who live in authenticity and without defences, and who are whole in what they think, feel, say and do.

Responsible, Not Guilty

When you free yourself of guilt, you live in peace within. You take on responsibility and stop martyring yourself with feelings of guilt. Taking on responsibility is constructive; it allows all your potential to remain awake and flow. You feel free and unburdened. When you get it wrong, you can find different methods to relieve yourself of the burden that it might imply.

For example, being sorry for or feeling remorse for something that you have done means that you are aware that you have acted against your own wellbeing or that of another. Realising it is good; it is the base for any positive change. The important thing is not to make a martyr of yourself. Learn the lesson. Say sorry, if it is the right thing. Put it right.

Remember that yesterday has already passed. The past cannot be changed. You can't swallow the words that you said, since you already said them. You can't repeat the scene from yesterday in a different way because it already happened and stayed recorded on the film of this eternal work. Therefore, don't repeat the words or the scene in your mind over and over again; doing that, you keep alive something that is dead, since yesterday already stayed behind. Learn from the error and commit yourself to you and to life, affirming that you will not fall over the same stone again. You will think about it before speaking or acting.

If there are people or situations that lead you to fall over the same stone, perhaps you will have to avoid them for a few days or a time, until you have strengthened yourself and have the inner security that they will not influence you. This is not running away; it is to be wise in knowing your weaknesses and knowing that to partake in similar situations is only to repeat the same errors and to worsen your wellbeing and that of the other. Trust in yourself. You can overcome these mistakes and stop making them. It is a question of loving yourself and living. Out of love, you stop hurting yourself and hurting the other.

Crying over the past, you don't mend anything. Open yourself to forgiveness. Raise the level of your thoughts so that they don't keep you in a state of sadness and loss of hope.

Don't allow your inner judge to sentence you each time that you act, since that way you won't feel free. Your judge that you carry within embitters your life; however, it is you that gives this judge the capacity to exist.

If the inner judge is in harmony with our conscience it is good, because it wants to protect us. On creating guilt it warns us that we have transgressed a rule of our code of beliefs, values or behaviours. It alerts us to the fact that we are acting against something important of ourselves. At those moments it helps us to observe and question what is real, true, important and even sacred in our life and for us.

The difference is between when we have established our own code of beliefs or conducts, and when we feel obliged to obey an imposed code. It is important for us to accept on an inner level the code by which we think we should be guided and act.

When we act out of obligation, by following a code of beliefs or behaviours that we feel have been imposed but aren't accepted as our own, we should ask ourselves why we act out of obligation, basing ourselves on a code we have not accepted. Are we perhaps afraid that, if we don't do it, we will feel guilty?

When we violate the codes of belonging to a group, family, social class or community, generally we feel guilty. If this guilt leads us to question ourselves about what is right for our conscience, we progress in our personal growth and improve our clarity.

It is necessary to respect ourselves, being clear about what the beliefs are on which we base our life, think, feel and evaluate. This will help us to avoid the excision between what we should and what we want to do. Until the *should* and the *want* are joined, we leave an open space for guilt. When we act according to how we feel we should, we will feel guilt for not doing what we want. While we act according to what we want, we will feel guilt for not doing what we should.

When guilt warns us that there is something to mend within us and we are willing to see it, dialogue and clarify, we are on the right path.

Sometimes guilt acts as an excuse for us to apologise without really taking on the responsibility for what happened; we deprive ourselves of the power to decide what we want in our lives and where to take it at each moment. We pass on the responsibility to the established norms, norms that in this case we haven't accepted as our own.

In any case, the antidote to guilt is to take on responsibility. And, when it is a matter of something that we could have done for someone and we didn't do it, let us recognise that we are not powerful enough to have been able to change the destiny of someone or something that happened. Remember, you can't change the past now. It was destined to happen. Stop lamenting it. Stop blaming yourself. Where you can, forgive; put right and learn. Grow with the experience.

Freeing Oneself from Anger

Rage has many 'offspring', such as hate, anger, intolerance, insistence, irritation, obsession, sarcasm, envy, the abuse of authority, impatience, the lack of forgiveness… Generally it 'explodes' when we want to control another or when our expectations have not been fulfilled.

Hate is an 'incendiary' emotion; it destroys the concentration and kills the capacity to act with dignity and excellence. You hate by justifying yourself in the other. You had expectations of them and they have let you down. They have wounded you and broken your heart. You answer this wound with revenge. You have to make them pay for it. You think that way you will do justice. This hate keeps you tied to the being that you hate. Instead of accepting them, forgiving them and letting go of them, you tie yourself to them more, nourishing the pain and the conflict.

Can hate be justified? Can it improve things? Can hate be healthy in any circumstance? Hate affects your health; it 'poisons'

75

your heart, kills your inner peace and dries you of love and happiness; you stay isolated in your aloneness, obscured by that rage.

Take a moment to reflect upon the last time that you hated someone. It might be difficult to see that your rage is created by no one but yourself. Although it 'seems' that the behaviour of the other person is responsible for your emotional state, the truth is that the hate is your reaction. Each answer that you create might be a conscious choice. You forget that you have the choice because it seems that the hate comes out of your inside in a natural way. In reality, you are allowing yourself to act driven by your automatic pilot, where your subconscious habits, which are based on your beliefs and your perception, form your conscious thoughts and actions. That is the sign of mental and emotional laziness; in that state, your intelligence 'sleeps' and it is impossible to think with clarity and take precise decisions.

To free yourself, you will have to take four important steps:

1. Understand that hate is not healthy. When you have a feeling of loss you feel sad. This sadness, because of the situation, generally precedes the feeling of hate, anger or frustration. Understand your emotions by observing them closely.
2. Accept that you are responsible for your own rage.
3. The other is free to act as they like, you can't change them, but you can improve your response.
4. Be prepared to observe, challenge and change the beliefs and perceptions that you base yourself on and that create your emotional pain. Some of these beliefs give force to your rage and block your learning. For example, when you think that it is good that you are angry, that to feel rage is the natural and normal reaction in the face of certain situations. Another belief is that anger causes the adrenaline to flow in you and you consider that it is a healthy addiction, that it makes you feel 'alive', that having sudden surges of adrenaline makes you feel

energetic and strong. You use any pretext (for example, the car parked double that didn't let you pass) to feel bad and, thanks to the car in front, your level of adrenaline rises!

Emotional suffering indicates to you that you have to change something in you, but you don't change anything. You ignore the messenger and the stress that you create continues to grow. Finally, it turns into such a habit that, if you relax and 'de-stress', you feel uncomfortable! You have got used to your stress.

Become aware of the need for you to evaluate your beliefs and their impact on your life. That way you will be more prepared to change and improve your habits. This is the first step to achieving it.

"It is impossible to get angry and to laugh at the same time," Wayne W. Dyer reminds us. Rage and laughter are mutually exclusive and you have the sufficient power to choose either of the two. Each time that you choose to get angry due to the behaviour of another person, you are depriving them of their right to be what they choose.

Overcoming Your Limits. Expressing All Your Potential

There are No Limits To How One Can Be, or Do.

I will give them a new heart and I will breathe into them a new spirit;
I will tear out of their body the heart of stone that they have now and I
will give them a heart of flesh.
Ezekiel, 11:19. The new Spirit promised to the exiles

A free being is the one who recognises their potential; they care for it, nourish it, use it and express it. It is an awakened being. It has stopped blaming, complaining and making excuses. It has taken on its full responsibility and has an attitude of gratitude at each moment. It is a relaxed being, but it does not get too comfortable in comfort zones or laziness. Out of serenity, it comes out of those spaces that limit potential to transcend and shine.

Its energy is full of love, courage and determination. It is a concentrated energy that governs their mind and emotions; it is not distracted by the trivial, it does not lose sight of the essential and does not allow itself to be trapped by anything or anybody. Therefore, their energy is fully centred and has great power. Not the apparent power that comes from stress, adrenaline, pride and the ego, but rather the power that arises from a being whose conscience, decision and action are aligned. From a being that knows that nothing or nobody can prevent it from being and being free.

Its mind is free and its heart is strong; it is a heart of light that does not wound, neither can it be wounded; it is not a heart of stone. Its motivation and intention is pure, clear and elevated.

Anthea Church describes to us the heart of an angel in a beautiful and profound way in *Angels* (1997): "The **heart of an angel** is a heart trusted by God not to hurt. Whatever happens, whether it is insulted or loved, it never hurts.

"The heart of an angel gives others courage to do what they have to do. It doesn't say 'maybe'; it says, 'yes… yes… you can do it.'

"The heart of an angel gives out to the world and takes only from God. It is the pivot point between the two. It is a place in which to recover, for in it only is nothing but love, and love heals. It is the crux of the soul and, if there is any ranking order in angels, it is based on the quality of the heart, for in the heart are the secrets that can make or break an angel's fortune.

"The heart of an angel is like a spirit on its own that can enter any place at any time because it frightens no one. Everyone says yes to an angel's heart, and when it enters, it sees only what is valuable and, stealing that to make the future with, leaves only fortune behind. And the fortune shines into the shadows and takes them away.

"An angel's heart is so deep that it does not alter. Whilst the body changes, the intelligence varies and strength diminishes, the hidden jewel of pure feeling that is an angel's heart lives through everything. And this is why it is the most precious entity the universe has... besides God, for whom in His uniqueness, the word 'value' doesn't apply."

Together with a heart like that, to live in freedom requires a free mind. **A free mind** is a mind without limits, open to everything and closed to nothing. It has all time available to it because it has managed to be above time. It is a mind that clings on to nothing and, because of this, is relaxed with everything.

A mind is closed because it gets stuck on something; it is blocked by fears or perturbed by worries. A person with a busy, closed and clinging mind will get perturbed, they will fluctuate, they will lose their emotional stability and they will be easily offended.

This doesn't happen to a person with a free, open and relaxed mind because they never lose sight of the authentic meaning of who they are. They don't lose themselves in a false identity, they don't identify with any role, person or situation. They maintain their identity, free of attachments, projections and identifications.

A person with a mind like that can use all of their creative capacity in order to live out their dreams.

To use one's creative capacity fully means:

- Being aware of the power of the imagination and channelling it in a constructive way.
- Being able and to be open to discovering, to marvelling and to learning.
- Becoming aware and dissolving self-limiting beliefs.
- Being attracted by excellence, embracing the experiences of superior quality and letting go of the desires and experiences of lesser quality.
- Having good discernment thanks to which one has a good

power of decision.

- Having the will power and discipline to apply decision.
- Having the courage to be different and to overcome obstacles.

Let's look at these points one by one:

The power of the imagination is extraordinary. The imagination is one of our greatest resources. It offers us many options and, with the clarity of our intuition and the power of our intention, we can use it to bring about marvelling, abundance and wholeness to our lives.

It is a matter of using the art of the imagination in a constructive way so that it does not betray us. The imagination should be at the service of our more healthy and positive intentions.

When the imagination is influenced by our limiting fears and beliefs, our mind begins to imagine the worst, to create scary scenes that end up by generating phobias and blocking us. Then we turn the imagination into an instrument to create fantasies that distance us from what is real. We believe in the fantasies that we have imagined and we project them onto reality.

The imagination has to be at the service of our being to help us to overcome our limitations and not the other way round, which would be when the imagination is at the service of our limiting beliefs and our fears, with which it weakens us and keeps us locked into the cages created by our own mind. From a grain of sand it imagines and creates a great mountain that prevents it from advancing, and this mountain only exists in its own mind.

When the imagination is at the service of the being, it is capable of turning a great mountain, a difficult situation, into a grain of sand.

There is nothing too big that the human being cannot overcome.

Discovering, Marvelling and Learning

When you discover, you open yourself to the new and you have the option of accepting some new information, a detail or new image. The discovery can be physical, emotional, mental, social, historical, artistic… That is, it can take on different dimensions. One that I find most exciting is the dimension of the invisible. From the East comes the idea of the third eye, of the spiritual intelligence that helps you to discover that which is invisible to the eyes but important and transcendent. When you discover it, perhaps it will turn into the essential, which will give a greater meaning to your existence.

You discover, out of curiosity, attention, passion, love and questioning.

Curiosity can lead you to a discovery that deepens your wisdom.

You discover thanks to being attentive, alert and open to new information and teachings. You discover out of love for people, nature and life and, when you discover, your life fills with a new energy that deepens your vision and your experience.

Being passionate about discovering a person is to take off their armour and see their essence.

To discover the essence of being, of objects and of life in general is to live life from a wide dimension in which creativity, beauty and opening form part of experience.

To discover means the courage to go within and see; to become aware of what is real and authentic. The fact of becoming aware is the basis for a change, to widen horizons and open yourself to a new way of seeing.

It is a new way of seeing where the observer doesn't lose himself in the observed. When we judge and we involve ourselves in others' stories, we get lost in them and our observation loses breadth and height. It is tainted by our emotional reactions and by our loss of serenity and mental peace.

It is a new form of seeing, free from the prejudices of the past, free of mistrust, fear and judgements, in order to look each other in the eyes, look at the soul, connect and listen without inhibitions. This connection between free hearts and between open minds is necessary if we want to transcend the barriers of racism, poverty and inequality that we have built.

Asking ourselves certain questions will help us to verify whether our beliefs and habits limit us. They are questions that allow us to open ourselves to discover and become aware of our ignorance and of the contradictions that prevent us from advancing towards the wholeness of our being.

Some of these questions would be:

- What do you want to achieve?
- What inner limitations prevent you from it?
- When you want to communicate something, are you able to say it as you want so that it has a beneficial effect on dialogue and the relationship? That is, do you have control and the freedom to express yourself?
- Are you free to understand yourself and others?
- Do you understand and accept yourself?
- Are you free to understand God?
- Are you free to transcend and draw close to the divine?
- What are your selfish desires? Selfish desires tie you. Pure desires, or we could say pure intentions and motivations, liberate you. Do they benefit you or do they tie you? Do they cause you more pain or more happiness? Why do you keep them?
- What are your pure intentions, what your soul really longs for?

Meditate to discover the answers, and to be surprised and marvel at your potential and all the beauty that lies in you and all that surrounds you.

Self-limitations

By nature, we are unlimited beings – transcendent. But we limit ourselves in comfortable zones. We get shored up. We act like fleas in a box: A man put some fleas in a box and the fleas jumped a lot. He covered the box and each time they jumped they hit the top of the box, and when they jumped too close to the right or the left they hit the sides of the box. Little by little they learned to jump just under the cover and without reaching the sides of the box. One day that man took off the top and opened the four sides of the box; he gave the fleas freedom, but they kept on jumping as far as the limit they had learned. In fact, the limits were no longer there. But they were conditioned. The same thing happens to us; we have a lot of conditionings that are, in reality, mental. It is within us to open the sides of the box and take off the top, or we can continue to live inside the box created by our own mind.

We act out of a complete inner mental freedom when we do not act under...

- Self-limiting beliefs.
- The negative images that we have created of ourselves.
- The sabotaging thoughts of doubt, which break trust in ourselves and do not allow energy to flow.
- The fear of failure.

Becoming aware of what our pattern of thoughts is that exercises a negative effect on us will help us to be free of it. While we do not become aware, we will remain asleep under its influence.

Let us look at some self-limitations:

Identifying Yourself With The Role

One of the reasons that we limit ourselves is because we identify ourselves with the role, that is, with the role that we play. In our thoughts, we maintain the image and the belief that we are the role. When something seems to threaten the role, we become

defensive. Identifying ourselves with a role or with a position limits us. According to the scenes and situations in which you find yourself, being free of labels allows you to act with greater freedom. For example, a manager can be a leader, consultant, colleague, monitor, coach, motivator or inspirer. To do so, one requires skills that one can learn and develop. It is merely a question of undoing the habit that limits you by making you believe that you can't.

Conversations with Yourself

The conversations that you hold with yourself – what you say to yourself – can liberate you or limit you. You can be self-critical and constructive, or judge yourself, threaten yourself and be destructive. You can support yourself or weaken yourself. When you talk to yourself, identifying yourself with a concrete role that supposes a limited vision, you lose control and get frustrated; anger comes up, and what you say to yourself generates conflict and weakens you. Learn to accept yourself, approve of yourself, whatever you do and wherever you are, and that way you break with the dependence of vision or leaning on others. Pay attention to your mental conversations.

Are You an Artist?

The word 'art' carries with it judgement values that, for many people, tend to become barriers. There is a good art and a bad art, fine art or noble art. All these terms evoke a finished product, a drawing, a painting, a piece of work or an object. Images, however, are a universal phenomenon that we all experience continuously in dreams, in the mind, when we listen to music or read a poem, even when we perceive an aroma that evokes a memory.

We all have internal images of our being, of those that we love, of those that we hate. Artistic creation is the process of giving form to those images. The traces that we leave during this process of

giving form do not have to be valued according to external criteria, but rather in accordance with our inner sense of what is true.

The creation of images is a way of breaking barriers, letting go of spent ideas and leaving room for the new ones.

The experiences of childhood include moments in which we create the impression that we were not and are not creative. Someone laughed at us at our first attempt to sing, write, draw or paint. That way, we came to the conclusion that we were not creative and since then we have avoided, as far as possible, any creative challenge in our life.

Remember that you are a born artist. Why? Because you think! Because you imagine! Because your memories and your experiences are full of images. Everything in life begins with the quality of your thought. Learning to think more creatively starts with accepting responsibility for all our thoughts and feelings.

Comparisons

When you compare yourself to someone, you want to be, have or do what the other is, has or does. It is as if you want to be another and not who you are. Your energy goes towards the other, instead of strengthening your talents, skills, possibilities and opportunities. Your jealousy and the fact of comparing yourself blind you to the possibilities that open up in front of you. Trying to have and be like the other, you are not grateful for what you have; neither do you accept who you are; you are never satisfied. This kind of dissatisfaction causes an unhappiness that reduces your vitality. Your energies stay limited and blocked.

Your Place in the Team

Some people feel comfortable being a player (member) of a team, others prefer to be sitting on the bench and watching the players; others prefer to work alone and think that team work is uncomfortable. Put yourself in a place where you feel uncomfortable and, on going through this discomfort, you will have an enormous process of learning about yourself. You will have to open up your limits, open yourself to new horizons and you will become aware of your possibilities. Finally, you will be able to be a team player, on your own or as an observer, according to the need and the moment.

You are Right

If you believe that you can, you are right.

If you believe that you can't, you are also right. Although you have the resources, the talents and aptitudes to be able to, if you have told yourself that you can't, you have closed off the possibilities for it to happen.

Without Limits

In some moment of our life we have had the experience of flowing without effort and of being in harmony with ourselves and the world (or the Universe). Generally it is an unforgettable experience. This experience is always possible. It is continually available, given that the full unlimited state of trust is always in you, just outside of your awareness of the routine of the day to day. It is a question of coming out of your inner self-created prison.

Embracing Excellence

When you have tried, experienced and felt something of superior quality, it is normal that nothing of a lesser quality attracts you. Perhaps it surprises you, because the people around you continue to be trapped by other kinds of desires and experiences that you are no longer attracted by.

You go onto a different plane of consciousness, and the inferior planes go to make up part of your past. Dare to live them. It is easy to lose direction; in that state, it is easy to feel and know what you have to do and, however, stop doing it. The most universal tendency is gravity, and it pulls downwards.

If you feel yourself to be influenced by everything that surrounds you and by the forces that pull you downwards, you stop living the extraordinary. You stop being inspiring so that many others also live it. You stay among the group of those who want to and do not achieve it.

When your experiences are of a higher quality, your consciousness is open to the universal, the unlimited, and you are not attracted by being trapped in things, objects, people, experiences or ideas for which, before, you would perhaps have given over your time, money, body and mind. Allow yourself to go towards, but not to cling to, this freedom that connects you and allows you to enjoy wholeness in the silence, in love and in true peace.

Discern Well in Order to Decide

In order to overcome our own limitations and have a more open and clear mind, we should pay attention to what we think, because the mind tends to jump from one place to another. It is convenient that there aren't thoughts that generate shadows, unhappiness, suffering and indecision; thoughts that the mind produces and that are useless or debilitating. All this clouds our own clarity. In order to change the direction of negative thoughts that generate fear and anxiety, we can strengthen the capacity to think positively. Try not to go round in circles with obsessive thoughts; try to think in a higher, concentrated way; that thought will have such clarity and force that it will help us to put it into practice more successfully.

What happens at times is that, when we don't trust in our capacity to resist pressure or difficulties, we feel ourselves to be insecure. A thought can block the capacity to feel whole and realised, and make us sad or irritated. A single thought can be the key to open the door that allows us to enjoy and feel the values of being. But it has to be a pure, strong, clear and concentrated thought.

To have good discernment, you have to know how to listen to the voice that you really want to listen to. There are many influences and inner voices that speak to you. There exists the voice of fear, of the ego, that of greed and the desires, that of the past, that of self-esteem, that of the values, that of your deepest dreams and longings, that of God, as well as the voices of the people that have relations with you and that advise you or give you their opinion. You listen to many inner and outer voices and, if you are not strong, your mind weakens under so many influences, which has, as a repercussion, a lack of clarity.

Because of all of this, on the one hand, you have to stay connected to the essential, and on the other, you have to strengthen your thought, that is, think less; think more slowly; more concentrated and clearly with sense, meaning and quality, based on a healthy and positive motivation. That thought is like an arrow; it has positive force and clarity. We can create this kind of positive thought with the practice of meditation, centring ourselves on creating affirmations that strengthen self-esteem.

The Will

The will leads thoughts, feelings, ideas, desires and needs to action. The will provides us with the motivation, the decision and the energy to act and do. When we incorporate the will into our life, we carry things out. We need will to achieve what we want to achieve. If we don't incorporate the will, the desires and ideas remain without being fulfilled. And we become part of that group of people who desire something and would like to achieve it but don't manage to.

The main barrier between where we are and where we want to be, between how we feel and how we would like to feel, is created by our mind. A mind that has transcended barriers and limits allows us to express all the potential of our being. It is a mind that allows us to be brave, to believe in our dreams and in being able to reach them. It is a mind that dares to think in a different way, takes the risk of failing and allows us to take on the freedom to be creative in order to change and shine.

The will and motivation, together with our intention, help us to knock down this barrier between what we would like it to be and what it is. They help us to make our dreams reality.

However, sometimes we feel 'defeated', de-motivated and with our will very weakened. Then faith, trust and courage come into action.

In the book *Dare to Live. Reflections on Fear, Courage and Wholeness* (O Books 2008), I devote various chapters to these subjects: courage, faith and trust.

Bravery and courage are the strengths that arise out of the heart of the being at different moments of life. Some need courage each morning to get out of bed and face the day. Others need it to take the next step in a relationship, whether this means reaching complete sincerity or getting closer or more distant. Some situations require a sacrifice on our part, and courage is the inner strength that will help us to take the step. It is the courage of the warrior.

We need courage to let go and to jump, perhaps, towards what seems to be a void; something or someone filled a space in our life, but the dependency and the fears that it carried with it are asphyxiating us. We need courage to let go.

When healthy intention, the will, courage, trust and faith go together, nothing and nobody can prevent us from realising our dreams, overcoming our limitations and living in wholeness.

Meditation: The Path Towards Freedom of Spirit

The meditator wants to reach the new at each moment, because with the new his intelligence is sharpened, and only with the new he himself is renewed. Only with the new is a path opened towards the definitive.

Osho: *Satyam, Shivam, Sundaram: Truth, Godliness and Beauty*

(1987)

The person whose spirit is free controls their mind, directs their thought and keeps their attention centred. Their heart is at peace, giving off positive energy and the energy of love; not the physical heart that pumps blood and makes it circulate, but the heart that is in the conscience – the heart of the soul.

It appears that many have left their heart in order to install themselves in the mind. On turning the mind into our residence, we stay busy by filling it with worries, anxiety, frustrations, angers and endless thoughts that agitate us and make us react. Like that, we are burying our true heart – the heart of the spirit.

Thoughts become a mist that prevents us from seeing and feeling with clarity. To the measure that these habits of accelerated thinking (the mind occupied and reactive) are fortified, our heart empties and stays hungry for the fresh air of love.

Other people have left their heart in order to reside not in their mind but in their intellect; they need to understand everything, analyse it, question it, justify it, reason it, conceptualise it, see it and touch it. Finally, their heart stops feeling, on remaining covered up by so much analysis and reasoning. For these people it is difficult to transcend conceptualisation and the language of the word in order to enter the kingdom of silence, beyond concepts and beliefs.

A third group of people do not reside in their mind or their intellect, but rather in their habits. They react in an automatic way, without thinking or reasoning. Their habits rule in their life. Their past has such weight that they live situations and relationships according to the habits that they have acquired on the way. They are trapped in the prison of their past. Their heart stops enjoying, since they live in the present in function of the past. Their personal history has such weight that their heart stops living in the present; it feels afflicted and stays hungry for the oxygen of love.

To reside in the heart of being and live life from this central space is to live awake to and aware of the reality that we are not our thoughts, our beliefs, our reasoning, or our habits. Our conscious being is metaphysical and spiritual energy. This energy moves and animates the physical energy of the body and the senses. From this central space, the heart of being, we direct the mind, the intellect and our habits.

The being has the faculties of the mind in order to think, imagine, dream, desire; the faculties of the intellect to analyse, reason, discern, decide; and the faculties of the archives in the memory, where the memories, beliefs, habits and conditioning are.

The awakened being is aware that **we are spiritual beings having a physical experience, and not physical beings that are trying to have a spiritual experience.** With the practice of meditation, the inner eye begins to 'see' another world without looking, and the inner heart begins to feel another world without touching. That is, it is an experience of seeing and feeling beyond the physical senses; you see and feel from within.

Meditation opens up the way for us to stop residing in the mind, the intellect or habits and reside in the heart of the conscious being. This being is like a star with five points; each one of the points represents one of the essential values of the soul; they are the values that make up the soul; they are its spine; the base that gives meaning to our existence.

Peace

Peace is serenity and not violence. It is to reconnect with harmony and to be at peace with yourself, with others, with what you do and with your past (if there is an aspect of your past that you haven't accepted, you will not be fine in the present moment; the past comes back to you once, twice or more times because you haven't reconciled yourself with your past). True peace is non-violence in all the areas of your life.

Purity

Authenticity, sincerity, honesty, transparency. In the present day we see that corruption, lies, and deceit abound because we have distanced ourselves from the heart of the soul and we reside in the periphery: in identities, roles and temporary and passing labels.

Love

True love is the love that is given to the other without desiring, without getting attached, without controlling, without the other person losing their freedom, or you yours. With meditation you learn to get back this dimension of universal love. You learn to value the self, the body, people and what you give to your body; your body is like the temple of the soul, you feed it better, you think better and you are more relaxed.

Innate Wisdom

Wisdom is our intuition, which guides us. When you connect to your intuition, you do not fail. You, being, are wise. How many times do we have an intuition to do something, but our logic, mind or beliefs say to us: "No, no! Not here! No! Over there."? Afterwards you think: "I should have done what I intuited?" We don't trust in this intuition because there are many mixes of selfishness, fears and opinions.

Freedom

The basis of happiness is true freedom; to feel the true wholeness of being; a wholeness that does not come from the outside in, but rather emerges and is transmitted from the inside out. The star is free and whole. In its authentic state, it lacks nothing of the essential. Each one of us is a star with five points. Each one of us is unique and we should not be afraid of shining, being unique and being different.

Meditation helps you to listen to the voice that harmonises with your being that is originally peaceful, authentic, loving, wise and free. In meditating you access the heart of being; the temple of being that has not been touched by pollution, fears, selfishness, greed, negativity, the useless or the superfluous.

Today, the word 'meditation' has a wide variety of interpretations. They range from the contemplation of ideas and concepts to an inner discipline of consciousness that seeks to reach enlightenment. Meditation is recognised as the path to integrating eternal truths into daily life and dissolving false beliefs and mirages. Meditation also goes together with prayer and devotion in some religious currents. In yoga, meditation comes in through physical postures, breathing exercises and as forms of learning to create mental postures that re-establish inner calm. In Raja Yoga, meditation is contemplated as the preparation of the consciousness for a union with the divine.

The practice of meditation helps us to tranquilise the mind, focus the attention, let go of wounds of the past, be fully present and heal the heart completely – achieving a great liberation.

It is a matter of going into the inner space in which there are no limits or frontiers. In it we find what we generally look for outside of ourselves. When you have reached that heart of being, it is like arriving home, at your real self. On arriving there, you realise that you have all that you really need in order to be happy; your state of feeling yourself to be a victim ends, and of being constantly needing, desiring and depending. At that moment you are a free spirit, and you are fully available to give to others.

Meditation is the journey towards the inside of your being, although, in fact, there is not a journey, given that your inner centre is a second away and at no distance from you. Therefore, you can access it when you like and wherever you are. With practise you learn to live IN this space and out of your spiritual heart. On relating to the world, you learn not to disconnect from your centre. You stay connected to the essential.

Meditation gives you the strength necessary to overcome obstacles and to get up after a fall. It helps you to maintain a healthy distance in order not to lose the 'eagle's' vision and to conserve the necessary detachment. In meditation you access all your potential of tenderness and you do not fear to open yourself to giving and receiving. You know that nobody can take away from you what you are, or wound your spiritual heart.

Meditation is a state of being, not only something that we do. It is the bridge that helps you to go from the theory to the practice. It brings you clarity, energy and discernment in order to realise your dream and your ideal. It helps you not to think too much, rather the right and necessary amount. When you think too much, the small things get bigger and turn into problems. With meditation you stabilise and learn to maintain the perspective of things; your thought fills with the power of pure energy, of trust and determination. That way you overcome the worries.

It is not a question of fighting, repressing or forcing your thoughts or feelings; simply learn to observe them, let them pass and, little by little, the mental noise will diminish. That way, you will distance yourself from the excess of mental work, from the constant occupation of the mind and you enter into the seat of being, where you allow the peace that lies there to invade your entire person. With this practice, you get over the addiction to action – to having to be doing something constantly.

Meditation offers multiple benefits that are scientifically proven. Even so, due to our addiction to action, we are incapable of seeing the value of sitting down for a while in contemplative silence. Our diaries are full of tasks, commitments and meetings. That way we avoid and postpone getting down to meditating. To do so, we use different excuses. One is that it is difficult for us to measure and evaluate the efficacy of the method. Another is that we expect immediate results. Another one is that it seems to us that we have to isolate ourselves and shut our eyes. Perhaps we think that we need a teacher, or to stop thinking, or for someone to give us a mantra, or that it will take us years to learn it and that it will be costly for us.

All of these reasons can be refuted, since they are not true. First, meditation that is done well offers results relatively quickly. It is possible to meditate in a group and with your eyes open. Someone can guide us in meditation, but we don't need a teacher. It is good to channel thought well and we don't need a mantra to do so. There are meditation centres that teach us the method free of cost.

In sum, there are no excuses for not meditating. We are only refrained by addiction, laziness and a lack of vision. Saying or thinking that we do not have time is not true either, given that the availability of time and how we use it is our decision. We are accustomed to pressurising ourselves; acting faster and faster and believing that we do not have time. Remember that, with practice, in a second you enter into your silent inner space. Do you have a second?

All you have to do is begin and experience it for yourself. On beginning meditation, you will realise that you find it difficult to hold your attention, concentration and deep reflection; the mind gets dispersed. For this reason, many begin to meditate but soon leave it. It needs mental discipline and perseverance. Creating positive thoughts and using them as affirmations that strengthen concentration and self-esteem can help when meditating.

Create an affirmation that you feel like feeling and living; for example, "I respect my intuition," "I have a clean conscience," "I am a being of peace," "I am free to be happy," "I can," "I am brave," "I am strong," "I trust," or "I accept and forgive." Let us be creative and generate a list of thoughts associated with the chosen affirmation, and let's visualise the associated feelings or images.

When meditating, we have to keep ourselves attentive, centred and alert. If we get distracted, we should return to the affirmation again. We have to be aware of what happens in the mind and actively distance it from the thoughts that distract it. We have to learn to let go of that which causes us suffering and encloses us in a spiral of painful thoughts and centre ourselves on the affirmation until we experience the positive meaning.

At the end of the book I include some meditations in order to begin the practice.

Being The Creator of Your Destiny

With Your Thoughts, You Create Your World

It is comfortable and pleasant to live with the old, but that will not bring you the flowers of freedom nor will it open up to you the whole sky for you to spread out your wings and fly. It will not allow you to reach the stars; it will not allow you to move in any direction or dimension. You will be like a tomb, in which nothing moves.
Osho: *Satyam, Shivam, Sundaram: Truth, Godliness and Beauty*
(1987)

With our actions, attitudes and behaviour, we transmit and give off energy. With each action we sow, and we have the full freedom to choose what we want to sow, transmit and give off. But, what we receive in return is related and linked to our sowing. We are free to sow seeds of trees of oranges, bananas or pears, but once we have sown orange trees we will receive oranges, not pears. As you sow, so shall you reap, the Bible tells us.

In terms of physics, Newton's Third Law reminds us that each action has an equal and opposing reaction. On the level of human energy, the law of karma is applied. Out of all the possible interpretations and explanations that we can give to the reality that we live as human beings, the one that has most sense, coherence and globality is the Law of karma. The writings of India 2,500 years ago spoke of it to us.

Natural laws govern our existence on a physical level and influence our lives. Understanding, in depth, how these laws function and work brings to us not only the power to change, but also the power to alter the course of our lives and really be the creators of our destiny. When we are aware of the law of reciprocity, we are much more cautious and attentive to the quality of energy that we give to others, independently of who they are or the situation we are in.

In order to live, we constantly carry out actions. They are always motivated by an intention, and imply an attitude and behaviour. According to the intention and the attitude with which you carry out an action, this latter will return to you in a beneficial, stressful, anguished or neutral way – the law says so. Nobody is exempt from the natural laws of cause and effect.

These laws function each time that you think, feel or act. For example, if you have a negative thought and you feed it and develop it for an hour, or if you get up in the morning with negative thoughts, this negativity will return to you. As a result, perhaps you feel depressed or angry, with rage, a headache, a weakened immune system, little energy and you have one of those days that you would prefer to forget.

Your thoughts affect the material, other people and yourself. Thoughts also affect the environment; children and animals pick up on the vibrations of others; perhaps they go spontaneously to a stranger or keep a distance from someone who is known to them. Someone commented to me that they did not trust a specific person, when I asked them why, they said: "Because the dog doesn't like them." Being in harmony with someone's vibration means that you pick up on the quality of their thoughts; a person with a good vibration thinks in positive and has careful thoughts; their attitude is congruent with this idea. On the other hand, a person with bad vibrations, perhaps, has a lot of anger, resentment or arrogance in their thoughts and attitude.

When you find yourself involved in a train of negative thoughts that lead you into a downward spiral, remember that you can talk to yourself and get yourself out of there. If you decide to carry out an action motivated by anger, jealousy, bitterness, hate or resentment, remember that this is what will return to you. If you do something kind for your enemy, you will help to dissolve the situation between you and them. If you keep up an aggressive position towards the other, you feed the situation and intensify the conflict. If you refuse to maintain an aggressive position towards the other, he or she will not be able to maintain it towards you. Two are required to create and maintain a conflict.

The Law of karma was imminent in Mahatma Gandhi's way of freeing India from the British government. His strict policy of non-violence and peaceful resistance guaranteed the victory according to the Law of karma.

According to the quality of your action, so will be the return. As we have seen, action is influenced by thoughts, the intention and the attitude. We could define three types of actions:

• Those that are impure, negative and murky.
• Those that are pure, positive and clear.
• Those that are neutral.

Impure actions are influenced by bad intentions, anger, bitterness, fears, rage, lust, attachment, greed, laziness, dishonesty, corruption, mistrust, etc.

Positive actions are influenced by good intentions and attitudes open to dialogue, to learning... They are actions ruled by compassion, forgiveness, love, happiness, peace, generosity, empathy, comprehension, trust, solidarity, etc.

Neutral actions do not imply either a negative or positive result. Everything remains as it was.

If you do something with the intention of benefiting someone but it does not give result, you will not receive a negative return, given that your intention was good. However, if you carried out an action with the intention of hurting someone, of 'making them pay', and that action did not hurt the other in the way that you wanted, even so you will receive the return of the vibration and energy that you have sent off into the Universe.

In our destiny we have to 'pay', or, in other words, we reap what we have sown or have thrown into the Universe, in our actions, attitudes and intentions. This is called paying off karma.

That is, to settle the accounts in order to clean the soul of the marks left on it by its negative actions or dark intentions. We also reap the fruits of the good seeds that we have planted.

There are many ways in which we gather the return of what we have thrown into the Universe. Let us remember that each action is an energy that we give to the world, and that energy returns to us in one way or another. We settle accounts through the body, the mind, finances, properties, time and relationships. We also settle them through what we call accidents or manifestations of the elements, such as droughts, floods, earthquakes, storms, volcanoes, tsunamis, extreme heat or cold, etc. All these manifestations show an imbalance that we have brought about with our actions that were motivated by greed, anger and selfishness.

Nature gives us signs that we have to change something, but, on not recognising them and not rectifying our direction, these signals turn into more difficult situations, harbingers of a greater imbalance and suffering.

Different spiritual traditions recommend to us how to purify the soul of accumulated negativity. For example, confessing and asking for forgiveness, from an understanding and willingness to change, or carrying out seva, that is, actions without the aim of gain; altruistic and without ambition of power or fame – helping one's neighbour out of solidarity, compassion and love.

To free oneself of the effects of negative karma it is necessary to live in accordance with the highest ethical and moral principles such as, for example, non-violence towards all live beings (this means being a vegetarian, given that it is an act of violence to kill and eat the flesh that embodies a live being), and Brahmacharya, which means purity in thought, word and action. Following a code of spiritual and ethical conduct has the objective of freeing oneself of lust, of the ego, anger, greed and attachment, and managing to realise positive actions.

For a westerner, these concepts can seem difficult to put into practice. However, practising them guarantees total freedom.

Mahatma Gandhi followed them assiduously. When they are embraced with true commitment, these spiritual guidelines carry with them a profound transformation and reduce the accumulation of negative karmic accounts.

The natural laws are irrevocable, which means that everyone is responsible for their actions. The laws of karma are not laws of punishment, at all; they are simply laws of cause and effect. They apply to our personal life, to our relationship with others, with nature and even with our own body. For example, if you nourish your body well, rest, exercise and take good care of it, your body will respond to you and you will have better health. However, if you eat fast food, drink alcohol, smoke, don't rest well, don't do enough exercise, your body, in the end, will return all this. The same thing can be said on a mental level: if you think and work maintaining a positive attitude, this is what will come back to you.

Understanding the natural laws of karma requires an in-depth study that goes beyond the aims of this book. It seemed important to me to speak of the subject, given that, to be free, we have to understand the responsibility and the limits of the freedom that we impose onto ourselves, according to what we sow, that is, and according to what we do and with what attitude and intention we do it. Understanding and being aware of these laws, we can better choose how to create our future and our destiny, and how to respond better to our present situations.

Judy Pemell in her book, *The Soul Illuminated*, explains to us the conversation that she had with one of the workers of a prison. She observed how patient, loving and kind his treatment was toward the prisoners. He was sincere, caring and tolerant on dealing with each one. His attitude stood out in all of the prison. He explained to me that he had carried out a sentence of more than twenty years for murder. They declared him the most violent person of the high security prison that he was in. The manager of the prison did not want him there, but had to keep him. The authorities did not know what to do with him. As a consequence, they decided he would be four years in isolation. This, he explained, gave him the opportunity to investigate into and think about himself.

When the four years finished, some people contacted him. He described them as very kind and full of compassion. This kindness and care touched him so much that he decided to write down all the things that he loved and considered so good in the people that were helping him. Then he wrote down all the things that he hated in himself. Finally, he took the decision to let go of all his negative features and behaviour and to take on the positive qualities of his helpers. From this moment, his mission was to share with other prisoners what he had received. That way he totally modified his destiny. On understanding the principles of the action, we are clearer as to how to change our destiny.

Amongst all the energies that can rule our life, those that have the greatest strength and power are the Law of reciprocity and the Law of karma. Nobody can free themselves of these laws of nature. However, there is an even greater power – the divine power; the power of the Supreme Soul; of God; of the Supreme energy, to whom many names have been given. The power of this energy is such that in a second, and for always, it can end negative features and behaviour, such as addictions. The only condition is that we hand ourselves over to it.

The more one lets go of negativity, the lighter one becomes, and the easier it is to connect to that Being of Light, since there is less interference of the personality. The more one links up with yoga, in union, the more one enters into a new interesting dynamic. In that spiritual communion a flame is lit and fed that generates heat. That heat, called the fire of yoga, burns the impurities of the soul. In the measure that this happens, the negative accounts are burnt and the soul is purified; it is cleaned and freed. Meditation is a powerful tool for the transformation of the self and to incinerate all the impurities that one carries within.

It is important to face the accounts of karma with humility, responsibility and with the will to finalise that account. If this means 'to bow down' (asking forgiveness, not continuing arguing or justifying your position, or leaving behind defensive attitudes) before those who oppose you, doing so will free you of the burden. If you don't do it out of pride, not only does the account continue, but it can increase and generate greater unhappiness or suffering.

Learning to accept, face and pay off our accounts is a passport towards freedom, wisdom and true happiness.

We could compare karmic accounts with a bank account. For each negative action, attitude and thought, the account is drawn from. For each positive action, attitude and intention and service the account is increased. And the account is mental, emotional, relational and physical.

Let us learn to add up and multiply positivity in our mental account, autonomy, love and compassion in our emotional account, kindness, solidarity and cooperation in our relational account and care, simplicity and respect in our physical account. For this, the first necessary change is that of the attitude. The second step is to improve and change our behaviour. The third is to change the most deeply rooted tendencies in the self, the habits and conditionings. The fourth is to improve our nature and personality. And finally, the consciousness experiences a lasting and permanent transformation. When we take the first step – improving our attitude towards the world, others and ourselves – we already experience the change of karma; we undergo an improvement of situations and all the elements that accompany them: money, relationships, circumstances and health.

Another factor that has to be taken into account is our response in the face of the destiny, the karma, that other people live. Sometimes, on protecting another person from the consequences of their own karma, we take on their consequences. A wise and knowing person will consider the effects of their actions in tiny detail before carrying them out. This implies having the sufficient power and vision to be able to foresee what the result of our actions will be, big or small.

Destiny is on a personal level, on the level of relationships and communities and also on the level of nations. We see it constantly in the news. Nations have a collective karma. We see it between the USA and the Middle East, between India and Pakistan, between Israel and Palestine. When the peace process fails and aggression increases, the account between the nations gets worse and escalates. With hostile demands, creating more adversaries, and following violent paths, this collective karma is worsened. When greed, economic control, racial or religious hatred feed the attitudes and conflict between nations and groups, the potential for devastation is incalculable.

It is easy to talk about the need for a new world order, but, who will bring this change in practice? The economists? The politicians? Will wars bring the change? The only real base for this new world order is the transformation in our consciousness; a spiritual transformation that means freeing ourselves of anger, lust, the ego, greed and attachment. Until this happens, the present world order will continue to rule, flooded in violence, suffering and arrogance. This is the karma of our contemporary world.

The transformation in our consciousness begins with allowing ourselves to be guided by innate wisdom. Wisdom will guide you on, not allowing you to be carried away out of reaction, the anger of the moment, the impulse of desire, or momentary pleasure.

If you are connected and centred in your BEING, your actions and answers will be guided by your highest values and that way you will be coherent in your life.

In order to take this first step – the change of attitude – we have to take charge of our mind. A mind that is clean, clear and free of dispersed and negative thoughts will help us to be transparent in our attitudes and intentions.

When you do something with a good intention but the other

does not perceive it, often it is due to the fact that our mind clouded over the intention (with doubts, dispersed thoughts) and/or the mind of the other was also clouded over. We have a 'radar' with which we perceive the intentions of the other, but often this radar is rusty or has interferences. It is a question of not allowing the mind to be dominated by unnecessary desires, negative habits or by self-limiting beliefs. The mind is the faculty that will help you to reach your destiny. If your mind is controlled by all this, you will not be able to be the creator of the destiny that you really want.

Meditation helps us to clean the mind of interferences and, thus, accumulate the necessary energy for transformation, allowing us to be the creators of the destiny that we want for ourselves and the world. Many have good intentions, but they lack the power and the energy to put them into practice.

In order to strengthen body musculature we need to do exercise with regularity and discipline and, in the same way, to recover our inner power we have to discipline the mind with exercises of positivity and silence. The less we think, the more power, light and clarity each thought will have and, therefore, the greater impact it will have on our reality.

Each one of us has the talent of the art of thinking, of imagining, of responding, of feeling, and in the same way that an artist has to refine his technique; has to practise and needs discipline, we, to develop these arts, also need to discipline our mind, control our thoughts better and guide them in the direction that will help us to be, do, feel and express our being better.

Once we achieve this control it is easier to control and create healthy attitudes in the face of our present destiny. That way, we take on the responsibility of recreating our destiny. The opposite would be to feel ourselves the victims of destiny, which causes us unhappiness, frustration and suffering, especially if what we are living through is not very pleasant; it seems that we feel ourselves to be a victim of a situation at which we have arrived through different circumstances and motives. Understand that you, at any moment, are capable of changing the situation or, if it doesn't change, you can change situation. That is, if you are in a place, with people, in a job, etc., where you feel uncomfortable and you believe that you need a change, you have various options: either you change the situation, and if it isn't in your hands, then you change situation. Alternatively, if you consider that you cannot change it or change situation, it is necessary for you to accept the situation as it is, not feeling yourself to be a victim, because you have chosen to be there. This requires a change of attitude.

We are responsible for what happens to us. What happens is that we don't always accept it. On many occasions, it is only when something 'big' happens to us that we realise that we have to change. Two hundred years ago, dying from a heart attack was a rare case – exceptional and worthy of medical study – now thousands of people die of cardiac arrest. We live at an unnatural rhythm. We are responsible for this, but we don't realise, or we don't want to realise it or take on the responsibility.

Taking on the responsibility means to accept the challenge of change. So, are you ready to embrace change? Do you have the will to work with whatever comes, to overcome it and change it? Are you prepared to continue to progress without it mattering what presents itself before you? Can you let go of what stops and breaks you in being the creator and ruler of your destiny and not its victim?

You Can

Direct Your Orchestra

When you direct your inner orchestra well, you can rule over external influences without succumbing to them. When the orchestra directs you, you dance from one side to another without a clear direction and with a melody that is not very harmonious; it is noisy and you suffer.

Our orchestra is made up of different music and instruments; memories, desires, tendencies, the mind, beliefs, culture, the emotions, feelings, fears, intuition, judgements, creativity, the imagination... Who is the director of this orchestra? You. Who are you? You – consciousness, you – the soul. You – being, the voice of your being, the voice that comes from the centre of the heart – of consciousness.

When your consciousness is in charge, you make the orchestra play according to the inner voice of your being, according to your intuition and your purest intentions.

You can.

You simply have to be awake, alert and attentive.

If the director of the orchestra closes his eyes for a few moments and covers up his ears, what happens to the orchestra?

You have to keep the eyes of your inner vision open; what is called the third eye. And LISTEN with your heart, not with your physical heart but with the heart of your being.

If your orchestra rules over you, and you – the director – are stiff, without flexibility, asleep, apathetic, you will not be able to achieve your dreams or arrive at the destiny that you would like to reach. And, to make things worse, when your orchestra dominates you, you are more vulnerable to being dominated by the orchestra of others. Or you let someone else direct your orchestra.

This is the ideal road on which to get trapped and suffer. Is this what you want?

You can direct your orchestra, which means that you can:

- Achieve what you want.
- Reach where you want.
- Be who you are.
- Stop being who you are not.
- Feel what you want to feel.

- Stop feeling what you do not want to feel.
- Be. You can be in your space.
- You can be present with all your being.
- Do. You can do what gives meaning to your life.
- You can stop doing what lowers you, is ordinary and you do not want to.
- You can reach excellence.
- Transcend.
- Live the essential.
- Let go of that which you have clung on to.
- Fly.
- Free yourself.

If you believe that you can, you can. You have to harmonise your inner voices. Listen to those that allow you power, strengthen you and accompany you. Silence the voices that repress you, judge you badly and limit you.

Inner Voices

The Voice of the Role
You are a responsible person. That is why you are reading this book. Your responsibility leads you to concern yourself with carrying out your roles and functions well. Does responsibility lead you to postpone the essential? First to fulfil it and then we will see? Then the 'after' never arrives, because there is always some responsibility or other to carry out and satisfy.

If this is what happens to you, add the following to your list of responsibilities: pleasure, wellbeing, rest, exercise, meditation, and the other essential things that your inner voice, of the role and responsibility of fulfilling it, prevents you from achieving. Give yourself this gift. Don't allow the voice of the work role or the family role make you put off the essential. Tomorrow may never come.

The Voice of the Judge

Your inner judge censures you, breaks you, limits you, judges you, makes you feel guilty, punishes you and represses you.

But, what is the function of your inner judge? It wants to protect you; it wants you to be good, prudent and precise. The voice of the judge feeds off your beliefs. You have to review what beliefs rule your inner life.

For your judge to carry out its function well – that of protecting you – it should base its judgements on the laws of nature, the laws of reciprocity, of karma, of abundance, of silence, the mental laws: the Law of cause-effect, the Law of attention, the Law of control, the Law of belief, the Law of correspondence, the Law of expectation, the Law of attraction and the Law of surrender. In the book *Who Rules in Your Life* (O Books, 2008), I devote a chapter to these eight mental laws.

When your inner judge bases its judgement on these laws, it stops being a judge and becomes your protector; you have managed to live in harmony with yourself, with others and with the Universe.

Write a letter to your judge. Tell it what you want. Tell it what you want it to stop doing and that you want it to support you, be your friend and help your conscience to judge well.

The Voice of the Creative

In you is the artist, the dreamer, that being with infinite possibilities of creativity. The voice of your inner artist wants you to break limits and jump over barriers to make possible the impossible, for you to transcend, to allow yourself to go beyond the social norms imposed by your 'clan' (family, professional, political, etc.).

The dreamer wants you to be free, for you to dare, to throw yourself into something and not to fear. The inner artist allows you to find different solutions than you would have imagined possible.

Does your artist live? Do you let the dreamer dream? Do you

listen to your dreams?

What relationship do the role, the judge and the artist have?

If the relationship is harmonious and they support each other, not only will your inner orchestra play extraordinary compositions, but you will be music for others; you will be an inspiration for those around you and you will feel well and happy, playing the tune that is yours to play and that comes from within you. It is your gift to the world.

When the voices of your different identities join together, when you resolve the fragmentation and internal division, you see and feel the unity not only in you but also in the Universe. Then you change the priorities that the system has taught you, those of producing and consuming, and you enter into creating and innovating. That way you develop your creative potential.

From this inner creative space, not only do you direct your orchestra, but you discover and transmit your special note in the great symphony of life. It is not a matter of looking for your note or your song, but rather of inviting it, waiting, being open and listening. Then you will know it. It is not someone else who will tell you how it should be. Only you know what it is. What is it that makes your soul and heart dance? Follow it.

Success or Failure?

You feel well when you realise that you are successful. However, when failure comes to you, you feel defeated. The definition of success and failure varies from one person to another and according to the stage of life that you are in.

It is important to have success and failure well defined for yourself, because, based on your definition, you feel greater or lesser wellbeing, happiness and wholeness. There are also different levels of success and of failure.

For example, for me the greatest success is to be happy and radiant, whatever happens inside or outside me. If I manage to keep happy in the face of failure, for me it is a success. Because to be happy means that I am connected with my essential worth, my being is awake and alive. Failure does not reduce vitality. The greater or fewer external achievements do not diminish the quality of being or of being happy.

The important thing is that you believe your own definition of success and failure. I am going to share some ideas that can act as guidelines, but, in the end, each person has to create and interiorise their own guidelines, factors and definitions of success and failure. Basing ourselves on these interiorised guidelines and beliefs, we evaluate our successes and failures.

For many, society has conditioned us to look for success through the path of our career, achievements, profits, applause and/or financial wealth. That way, we have learned a narrow view of success. Running in search of this kind of success and pursuing it, we come to exhaust ourselves, get burnt out and depressed. In order to achieve these successes we have stopped caring for the being and relationships. That has meant and means stress, anguish, anxiety, family break ups, personal and relational disintegrations, the destruction of the environment and planetary and climatic imbalances. As a consequence, we feel empty. Although we achieve the applause, the income and other successes, the soul is malnourished and has the sensation that it is lacking something.

Reaching fame, financial wealth, the power of a visible position, and reaching it with a broken soul, broken up family and a sick body, causes a depression which explains why, in our recent history, famous people have ended up committing suicide.

Mike George (*Clear Thinking*, number 66) tells us an interesting story in which he shows the contrast between success understood as a career of achievements in order to then 'have time' and success based on the culture of having enough, relaxing and enjoying. It is the story of a fisherman who leaves early to fish each morning. At eleven in the morning he has already picked up enough fish to cover his needs and then he rests quietly on the beach. A tourist who is walking on the beach sees the idyllic scene: a man, dressed in simple clothes, resting on a fishing boat on the beach. The tourist sits down next to him and begins a conversation. "The weather is extraordinary. There is a lot of fish. Why are you lying here instead of going to fish for more?" The fisherman responds: "Because I have already fished enough this morning." "But, imagine," continues the tourist, "that you could go out to fish three or four times a day, bringing in three or four times more fish. And do you know what you would achieve then? In a year you would be able to buy yourself a motorboat, in two years you would be able to buy yourself a second boat and by the third year you would be able to have a much more powerful boat until, finally, you would be able to build a frozen foods plant or a plant for smoking fish; perhaps you could have your helicopter in order to follow the shoals of fish and guide your boats to fish more. Perhaps too, you could have lorries in order to take the fish to the capital and then..." "And, then?" asks the fisherman. "Then," continues the tourist triumphantly, "you would be able to be sitting quietly on the beach, sunbathing and looking at the beauty of the sea." The fisherman looks at the tourist: "But that is exactly what I was doing before you turned up."

If we want to redirect our personal and collective lives toward a true wellbeing and wholeness, we have to re-evaluate and redefine our beliefs and factors of success and failure.

Before asking yourself what success and failure mean for you, it is important to be clear what context you want success in. Depending on the context, the dimension and the meaning of success and failure will be different. For example, in the work context, a failure will be different to in the family context. In the personal context or in life in general, the way of perceiving success varies.

In one of my seminars we did a task with sixty participants in order to define success and the factors that lead us to it, and to define failure and the factors that cause it.

Here are the conclusions:

Definition of Success
- Moment of inner wholeness. Feeling yourself whole, full of happiness, with an optimistic mental state, without fear, happy and in a good mood. Being fine, in balance and at peace with oneself.
- Finding meaning in what you do.
- Discovering what will bring you closer to your dream.
- Success is about more than just having; it is facing all situations, even the negative ones, transforming them into the positive and feeling yourself realised, personally and emotionally.
- Having courage to take forward what you want, in spite of what you find against it.
- Achieving in each moment the desired objectives on all levels of being. Fulfilling set objectives and adopting a positive attitude.
- Being able to be beyond noise.
- Humility of the self.
- Not being afraid of failure.
- Satisfaction at work.
- Coherence with oneself.

Factors That Bring Us Closer to Success
- Appreciation.
- Gratitude toward oneself and others.
- Acceptance.
- Self-esteem.
- Trust.
- Constancy.
- Courage and determination.
- Integrity.
- Honesty.

- Believing in what you do, regardless of external factors.
- Responsibility, feeling yourself realised, work well done.
- Work, dedication, determination and tranquillity.
- Being positive in the face of adversities.
- Being consistent with your values.
- Precision in decisions and choices.
- Focus.
- Doing it with love.
- Giving the maximum of yourself.
- Being provocative.
- Creativity.
- Thoughts and emotions in line.
- Staying happy and laughing at yourself.

Definition of Failure

- According to perception: failure does not exist, it is learned.
- An opportunity to recognise mistakes; overcoming, at each moment, the problems that life sets in front of you and turning them into challenges.
- Staying stuck in what you could have done and haven't done.
- Frustration, pain, suffering.
- Not understanding.
- Not controlling violence.
- Having lost your notion of the dream, of the ideal of life.
- Not fulfilling set expectations and not knowing how to accept it.
- Not having enough courage and bravery to walk through life.
- Not being the ruler of your life.
- Allowing yourself to be led by something negative that a particular situation causes.
- Distancing yourself from your values.
- Being incongruent.

- False expectations.
- Excessive attachment.
- Materialism.
- When the self does not accept what life brings it.
- Putting your life in the hands of, and blaming, others and circumstances with feelings of emptiness and confusion.

Factors that Bring Us Closer to Failure

- Ignorance.
- Despondency.
- Disillusion.
- Fear.
- Confusion.
- Influences.
- Mental weakness.
- Insecurity.
- Inexperience.
- Ego, arrogance.
- Mistrust.
- Attachment, dependencies.
- Excuses, laziness, putting off.
- Excess of acceptance with submission.
- Fear of being yourself and shining.
- Making judgements without an objective vision.
- False perfection.
- Believing that we are always in the possession of the truth.
- Nervousness.
- Not taking on limits.
- Low self-esteem.
- Blockages. Not going forward.
- Intolerance.
- Rigidity.
- Cowardice.
- Lack of coherence.

You can reflect on what true success and failure mean for you and, according to those meanings, centre your attention on the values and efforts that lead you to achieve your objectives.

Living Out Your Purpose and Re-connecting to Your Dream

And Jesus said: 'My brother, your thoughts are wrong; your heaven is not far away; and it is not a place of limits and bounds, it is not a country to be reached; it is a state of mind. God never made a heaven for man; he never made a hell: we are creators and we make our own. Now, cease to seek for heaven in the skies; just open the windows of your hearts and, like a flood of light, a heaven will come and will bring a boundless joy.

Levi H. Dowling, *The Aquarian Gospel of Jesus the Christ* (1910)

Our dreams are our paradises. Living out our dream is to live our paradise here and now. If everything that we do during the day and in life is directed at fulfilling our purpose – our reason for being, for existing and for living – we will be much happier in everything we do, because everything will be channelled towards what we really want. On the other hand, if we do a little bit of everything, but without knowing where we are going, we will be like a shipwrecked person who moves steering along but now goes towards the right, now to the left, goes backwards, towards the north, towards the south and in the end stays in the same place and gets nowhere, although they are working all the time. It lets itself be carried by the currents, the tides, the waves and the winds. It has lost its bearings and doesn't know how to be guided by the stars. It has left its consciousness asleep and doesn't listen to intuition.

We all always have something to do, something to say and/or something to think about. We are occupied. The question is whether everything that we do forms part of our life purpose or whether we are simply occupying time and using our energy in tasks and conversations that do not lead us to anything transcendental or whole. We simply pass the time doing and talking, but without a sense of purpose. Although the things we do and/or speak about are necessary, if they do not make up part of our life purpose, they will exhaust us. We will feel an inner emptiness and dissatisfaction, as if we are missing something.

The most authentic purpose is that of fulfilling our ideal, our dream in life. What happens is that, sometimes, we haven't worked out what our purpose or life ideal is.

We have to ask ourselves what our true purpose is. There is a purpose related to oneself and one related to what we want to offer to the world. During the day we are exchanging, therefore, we have something to give to the world; each one of us is different; we can play our note in order to contribute to the symphony of the Universe.

A question that can help you to find your purpose is: when you feel whole, when you feel on top form, when you feel full of enthusiasm, what is there in you? Who are you at that moment? How do you feel? What do you give to your surroundings and to others? This is something that you want to reach and keep. Ask yourself that question. Visualise that moment, which at some time in life you will have experienced. If not, visualise what you would like to experience. Go there seeing in what way this connects with what you would really like to reach, as a person, as a being.

Second question: how can you transmit it to the world? What is it that you want to transmit to others? What is it that you want to give? That is, what do you want to devote yourself to? This isn't limited to a profession, but rather applies to what you offer and transmit with what you do in the day to day, in relationships, with people, with the daily manifestation of your thoughts, words and actions in the family, at work, in the supermarket, with friends, with acquaintances and with strangers.

To carry out this inner inquiry you need to go to its deepest part. What is your purpose? Not your purpose in that this weekend you want to go to this seminar or not, or that in the holidays you want to go to Thailand; all these are short term purposes. Your life purpose refers to what it is that you really want to reach. If you clarify it, it will help you to make decisions with clarity and determination in your life.

We are constantly making decisions, but many times we do it according to circumstances, the moment and how we are, but not according to what we really want to achieve. We go against ourselves because our decisions are not in line with what we really want. When we don't know what we want, we allow ourselves to be influenced.

It is a matter of re-connecting with our dream and living out our purpose. The dream is the life ideal, that which motivates you and moves you. The dream is that for which you would give your life. The dream, in general, is utopian. On occasions, we have believed in our dream but then it broke, and on other occasions we have stopped believing in the dream because the reality of the day to day is 'hard' – it is not always hard, but we live it as if it were – it is difficult, complicated, complex, and seems as if one thing is what the reality of the dream could be and another is day to day reality.

Re-connecting with the dream is to do so with what really makes you beat, with what really moves you. It is what makes your soul and your heart dance on a profound level, on an existential and life level, not a momentary passion, emotion or activity of a night, a party, a relationship, but rather something deeper and more lasting.

The dream is the life ideal into which all the pieces of the jigsaw of your life fit. If you forget that life ideal and live reality from the daily, the ordinary, the routine, what you have to do out of responsibility, because you have no other choice, then from that attitude comes fear, apathy, laziness and resistances. There is fear of change, of leaving behind the reality that you live in and creating another different and daring reality;

we get used to one reality and we resign ourselves to living as victims of that reality. When this happens, we lose our spark, our happiness and our magic, and we do not bring our difference to the symphony of life.

Each one of us has something to bring (talents, capacities or creativity) and we can give our touch of difference, not with the objective of standing out or being famous; it is a matter of finding what your quality is; your talent; your speciality; your virtue; the inner strength that you can bring to your reality, to what surrounds you and the world.

Setting ourselves objectives will help us to channel all the potential that we carry within and have achievements that go beyond what we would have imagined to be possible.

Everything that we do is propelled by an intention and motivation. It can have, as an end, the mere fact of satisfying a need, a desire or an addiction, or, instead, it can be driven by the desire to reach an objective, a purpose, or a more intangible dream.

We have various energies that put our engines for action into gear. Let us see some of them:

- Necessity.
- Desire.
- Dependence/addiction.
- Expectation.
- Ambition.
- Objective/goal.
- Vision.
- Purpose.
- Dream.

All these factors move our energy in order to go into action.

Necessity
They are very practical aspects, necessary to subsist. For example,

we eat in order to give the body the calories necessary to move and live. Hunger generates that necessity.

Desire

There are many types and levels of desire. Desire is a great driving force. There are desires brought about by greed, lust and attachment. They are desires that leave us constantly dissatisfied, given that, even when we manage to satisfy one, it reproduces and engenders ten more desires. The chain of desires that greed produces is unending.

The desires brought about by anger and bitterness engender violence and destruction. They are desires that cause unhappiness, non-union, imbalance and suffering. In fact, they arise from an inner space without harmony.

There are desires brought about by values such as love, sincerity and respect.

In essence, we have to review the nature of the seed from where our desire sprouts. If the seed is good, the desire will lead us to cultivate it and to achieve good fruit.

The Bhagavad Gita (3, 9) tells us, "carry out your actions with purity, free from the slavery of desire."

We shouldn't allow the limited and momentary desires to distract us from our true objectives and make us lose sight of our life ideal and our dream.

Dependencies and Addiction

Dependencies often lead us to act, even against our will. We have become puppets and have offered the strings to another, who pulls them. We act and move without wanting to move like that. We are dominated by fear and dependency. When this reaches its extreme, it becomes an addiction. Out of addiction we do things that destroy our integrity and our health.

We pursue the object, the person, the pleasure or the substance that we are addicted to and our reasoning stops advising us correctly. All this leads us, in the end, to a deep sadness, which, at times, is so difficult to admit and live through that one increases one's dependency and addiction in order to 'cover over' or flee from this deep sadness. It is a dead-end road; a spiral that takes us down and the consequences can be horrible.

Leaving the atmosphere that has led us to this state, a strong will and accepting help are some of the factors that can help us to get out of this dead-end road and change direction; re-find the way and come out of the dark night to enter into the dawn.

Expectations

When we do something, we do it with the expectation of achieving some results. The expectations generate anxiety in us when the results do not arrive.

To conquer this, it is a matter of being capable of aiming ourselves at our objectives and dreams without the expectation of them being fulfilled now, or on a specific date. If not, we live in function of tomorrow and we don't enjoy today. It is essential to have a balance between planning, the calendar and the dates, and the knowledge that you are doing what you should and what you can to achieve these objectives, but you don't allow your happiness to depend on achieving them. If your happiness depends on your achievements, you will always delay it. **Happiness is not later, it is always now**. We need to learn the art of having some clear objectives but not getting upset or discouraged if we don't achieve them 'in time'.

Ambition

Healthy ambition leads us to transcend ourselves and make an effort to go beyond our limits.

When ambition is linked to power, position, money, posses-sions and prestige, it can become harmful for our being. We stop looking after ourselves in order to achieve what is out there. What is out there takes on more importance than what is within. The soul empties and life 'dries up'. It loses love, tenderness and wholeness, and gains in anxiety, stress, anguish and fear.

Objectives and Goals

Objectives are made up of one or various goals that we fix with certain actions that have to be carried out. We plan them with clarity and we allocate them in a concrete time and space.

Vision

A vision takes on many forms. There is a historical vision, to know where you have been, a situational vision, to see where you are and a strategic vision, to find out the direction you should be going in. The strategic vision can be based on tendencies or present models of functioning that can continue to be used or integrated in the future, or it can be an intuitive awareness of what it will be.

A vision is also what we visualise and what we would like to achieve. A vision is wider and more abstract than an objective, which is more concrete and limited in time and space, with defined actions and places.

The Purpose

The purpose is your reason for being, for living and for existing. **Your purpose can be to live your dream instead of dreaming your life.**

The Dream

A dream is also a vision that contains aspirations, sometimes so elevated that they touch on the impossible. If you believe in what you imagine and create – if you believe in your dream – you will achieve it.

A dream shouldn't become a fantasy or escape. This happens when we have conceived the dream, but we do not believe in it, ourselves or destiny. We lack conviction. By nature we are unlimited, but we have already seen that we have beliefs and attitudes that limit us. **Living our dream is to dare to live one's being without limits.**

To live your dream is to live your life ideal. It is to live what gives meaning to your life. You live beyond what is vulgar, mediocre and ordinary. Even in small tasks you give the touch of your greatness, of your special note. You go beyond ordinariness, without stopping your participation in the ordinary and necessary; you keep in your soul the eagle's vision, above; you don't lose sight of the great picture. You love, you enjoy and you help from this state. You place yourself in the sacred space from which you live your dream.

Your sacred space is peaceful, clean, clear, strong, loving and secure. It is a space that allows you to access your inner wisdom. In it you trust, you charge your energy and you live connected to your life ideals.

To re-connect with your dream you have to ask yourself what it is that you really desire in life. In Anthony Robbins' book, *Awaken the Giant Within,* he sets out how to resolve this question: "Ask yourself what you truly want in life. Do you want a loving marriage, the respect of your children? Do you want plenty of money, fast cars, a thriving business, a house on the hill? Do you want to travel the world, visit exotic ports of call, see historical landmarks firsthand? Do you want to be idolized by millions as a rock musician or as a celebrity with your star on Hollywood Boulevard? Do you want to leave your mark for posterity as the inventor of a time travel machine? Do you want to work with Mother Teresa to save the world, or take a proactive role in making a measurable impact environmentally?

Whatever you desire or crave, perhaps you should ask yourself, 'Why do I want these things?' Don't you want fine cars, for example, because you really desire the feelings of accomplishment and prestige you think they would bring? Why do you want a great family life? Is it because you think it will give you feelings of love, intimacy, connection, or warmth? Do you want to save the world because of the feelings of contribution and making a difference you believe this will give you? In short, then, isn't it true that what you really want is simply to change the way you feel? What it all comes down to is the fact that you want these things or results because you see them as a means to achieving certain feelings, emotions, or states that you desire".

Working to change and improve how we feel can be something that drives us to make an effort and visualise where we want to arrive. However, living our dream implies knowing how to control our inner states, so that our feelings and sensations do not depend on passing or temporary factors, such as the moods of another person or our own, circumstances or time.

Sometimes, instead of living our dream, we dream our life. Instead of living our life ideal – what motivates us – we resign ourselves to living life from routine, from the ordinary and even from the mediocre. We have lost the elegance, the nobility, the sacred, the magic, the different and we fall into an automatism. In this automatism we lose the connection with our true being and our purpose.

Instead of living on automatic pilot, bring your dream to practical life and incorporate your ideal into each situation that you are creating. It is good to do an exercise: each morning, ask yourself over several days, "Does what I am going to do today motivate me? Does it fill me with enthusiasm? Do I want to do it?" If over various days, when you wake up, the answer to this question is no, ask yourself what you are doing. Change something, because you ought to wake up with the joy of knowing that you are going to live your dream.

Take the example of the story of the birds who make their nest, and although it is destroyed, they make it again and again. They firmly believe in their purpose. The story says thus: Have you observed the attitude of birds in the face of adversity? They spend days and days making their nest, collecting materials sometimes brought from long distances. And when it is finished and they are ready to lay their eggs, the inclemency of the weather or the work of the human being or some animal, destroys it and throws to the ground what they achieved with so much effort.

What does the bird do? Does it stop, abandoning the task? No way. It starts again, once and again, until the first eggs appear in the nest. Many times before the chicks are born, some animal, a child, a storm, destroys the nest again, but this time with its precious contents.

It hurts to start from zero… But even so the bird never goes silent or gives up; it continues singing and building, building and singing.

Have you felt that your life, your work, your family or your friends are not what you dreamt of? Have you wanted to say, enough, the effort isn't worth it; it is too much for me? Are you tired of starting again, of the exhaustion of the daily battle, of betrayed trust, of goals not reached when you were on the point of achieving them? Even though life hits you once more, never give up, get your hope back and get down to the task… And, above all… never stop singing.

Remember and ask yourself what your purpose is. What is your dream? That which makes you fly, that makes you happy. I am not referring to something momentarily passing, like an ice cream that you eat and after a while the taste and sweetness of the sugar, chocolate or vanilla has dissolved. I am referring to the main thread of your life, to something that you feel passionate about, that motivates you, that fills you with enthusiasm. Dare to live it.

If you resign yourself because there are obstacles, because it is difficult or because you are not understood – think; do you really want to live your ideal? There will always be obstacles. You have to be like the river that, although it finds a mountain, knows it has to reach the sea, and travels around the mountain to do so. We find ourselves with the mountain and we get stuck. We think,

"Oh, this mountain is in my way and I can't move it! How am I going to reach the sea? I'll stop trying to reach the sea. I'll put up with the reality that a mountain has appeared in my life – perhaps it is my destiny! The thing is – I can't do anything! The mountain is very big!"

You begin to reason about everything that has got in the way on your path, as if to kill the dream. Then you turn into a pond – a puddle. Like stagnant water, you no longer flow towards the sea. Why have you allowed the mountain to cover up your dream? The mountain can mean many things.

To live your dream and your purpose is to dare to break with the image that others might have of you, with the expectations that they might have of you, with the habits, the conditioning, what you are accustomed to; in other words it is to dare to be different and to be yourself.

Our purpose is to live from the heart, that for which we were born and why we are here. Were we born and are simply here to suffer and to try to get ahead? Life has magic, it has colour. Let's live it!

Going on with the example of the river, what is the purpose of the river? As well as having the aim of reaching the sea and melting into it, the river nourishes everything that it touches on its way. Wherever a river flows, everything receives nutrition – the grass, the flowers, the trees and all those who go to its banks to nourish themselves from its waters. The river cleans and nourishes as it passes.

This can suggest to us our highest purpose – it is not only to reach a concrete destiny, but to share, collaborate and nourish others and nature, animals and the planet, with our presence. It implies changing our consciousness; instead of wanting to take from everybody and everything that we find as we pass, having the awareness to give and share. It is to go from being a mere consumer to being a giver. In fact, when you want to take from the other, you throw the message to the Universe of, "Give me, give me love, give me respect, consider me, I need, I need, I need," and at bottom, you are saying that you don't trust that what you need will come unless you ask for it like a beggar. You can formulate the intention of what you want, but it is out of your dignity and self-respect that you will receive it, without a doubt.

From the awareness of the 'beggar' in which you believe that you do not have and need, you say, "Give me, I want, I desire." You fight for it; it seems that you transfer your value and the meaning of your life to having and possessing, not to being.

In the metaphor of the river, we live from abundance. The river gives, shares, nourishes, doesn't discriminate and flows. The river trusts that it will be nourished and lives in the awareness of abundance. The question that you can ask yourself, to change from the 'I want and I need' to giving and sharing is: "How can I help? What contribution can I make? What significant change can I bring?" The intention to serve and contribute will reveal and clarify what the need is and what you can bring. Your heart will become more generous. Your mind will widen frontiers. Your vision will cross horizons. You will realise that, on serving and helping, your life takes on another meaning. If you don't find meaning in your life, open yourself to collaborating, helping; become a volunteer, and you will see that, on giving yourself to others, you receive their affection, appreciation and love. All of those are blessings for the soul. The soul, thus, leaves its saddened and stagnated state and begins to flow like the river that nourishes all those with whom you enter into connection.

There are moments in our life in which we ask with greater clarity the meaning of everything that we are doing and living. In maturity, when we have established careers, formed a family and years of experience, we usually enter into a radical questioning. Do we want to continue with the same person and the same work until the end of our life?

I have many friends and acquaintances that, between forty and forty-five, have left their jobs to set up their own company, separated and divorced, and have begun a spiritual path... In sum, their life has taken a great turn.

There are other moments that also lead us to ask ourselves about the meaning of our life and our true purpose:

- Illness.
- The loss of a daughter or son.
- The loss of a loved one, partner or friend.
- Being faced with death.
- On experiencing a great disappointment or frustration.

As Francesc Torralba reminds us in his book, *The Meaning of Life*, thinking about death offers us the opportunity to redesign our life project. Meditating on our absence is an occasion to value our presence more.

There are moments in our life when we are connected to our deepest ideals and dreams, but then it seems that one or various curtains cover up our vision and we stop seeing and living that motivating energy that the dream provides us with.

Some of these curtains are related to the self-limiting beliefs that I wrote about in the section, 'Self-limitations'. Others have to do with our tendency to intellectualise everything – put labels on everything. This distances us from the innocence and freshness of a clean and non-judgemental look.

Faced with a baby, we let go of our defences and pretensions; the curtains open and we get back to the space of innocence of one who doesn't even know what it is to feel itself guilty. The energy of the baby is clean, pure, without mirages and fills us with trust because the baby is born in the trust that the Universe will give it what it needs to be fed, grow and become. **In the presence of a being without defences, we take down our own. We leave behind the mirages, pretensions, labels and other limitations and we enter into a space full of sincerity and authenticity.**

As well as babies, there are other beings who have the capacity to take us to this space. They are wise people, saints, gurus, monks; people who have spent years freeing themselves of mirages, false beliefs and the conditionings of the world, and have returned to their state of original, pure and innocent being.

What are the steps that we should take in order to live our dreams?

Our dream can focus on the here, the now and our inner self. Another option is when we focus our dreams on achieving things 'outside of us'. It is interesting to join both directions: towards within and towards without. It is to set out to ourselves what we want to achieve outside us and what we want to achieve within us.

We begin by reopening the meaning of our life and asking ourselves what we want. Then we have to propose to ourselves with sincerity, bravery and effort the beginning of the steps to achieve it. Without this will, we will give up at the first obstacle. What is more, we have to stay aware and keep the vision of our goal in front of us, since on the path we are presented with many distractions and deceptive purposes.

For example, when you find yourself with someone who has what you don't have and has achieved what you haven't achieved and they seem happy, in a more or less unconscious and automatic way, the desire to have what they have arises in you – you compare yourself; you stop valuing what you have and begin to want what the other has. If you also believe that they are happy because of what they have, you fall into the trap of wanting it too; a trap because happiness does not come from what you possess, but rather from who you are and your capacity to share that with others.

So, to sum up, these first steps are to begin to know what you want, second, to set out in yourself firmly to achieve it and third, to keep the intention and clarity not to go off the track.

On asking yourself what you want, you can listen to the call of your heart, the call of time, the call of your loved ones, the call of humanity, the call of the planet and the call of God. The fact of listening to the answer of each one of these calls can widen your horizons and give your dream a wider and more transcendent dimension.

To live your dream, you need:

- To believe firmly in it.
- Flexibility to go round the mountains and jump over the stones and barriers, not to insist on wanting to knock down the mountain with a hammer in order to go straight according to the path that you had set. Be flexible.
- Inner power to not get discouraged.
- Detach yourself from the results; if they come, you are happy, if they don't come, also. Remember: happiness comes from within and is expressed outwards. Happiness is now and not later.
- Let go of the past. Don't cling on to your personal history. Don't want to relive the applause received yesterday – that distances us from the here and now.
- It helps us to know how to turn our dream into a necessity and a priority. In the same way that we eat out of necessity, it is a priority and necessary to live our dream in order to nourish the soul. A nourished soul can nourish the world.
- When what surrounds you, your circumstances, people and places, seem to distance you from the destiny that you want to create and live you have to ask yourself again if you want to continue there, not resign yourself and 'kill' your dream. If you do so, your soul will wilt. Review why you have reached where you are now; it is your decisions and actions that have brought you here? If the here is in contradiction with the life purpose that you have, ask yourself again what you are going to do from now on.
- You have to love what you do. As Leo Tolstoy said, "The

secret of happiness does not lie in always doing what one loves, but rather in always loving what one does."

We are living in an extraordinary moment of the history of humanity. It is the end of the night and the beginning of the dawn. The dawn has already begun. The darkest moment of the night is just before the dawn breaks, before the daybreak – we are in this moment. Some are trapped in the darkness but others are living the sunrise and making it come out in them. It is not a dawn from the outside; it is a dawn of human consciousness. To live our dream is to live this dawn; it is to live what gives you light and connects you to your light.

To live it sometimes means a rupture; a rupture with a place, a past, a relationship, some beliefs, a job or a profession, amongst other possible ruptures. This rupture perhaps generates unhappiness, but you can do it with elegance, knowing that you are breaking limits, opening yourself and reconnecting with your life ideal. From this awareness, that rupture doesn't generate as much suffering as it could generate if it were living without a wide and transcendent vision.

On the other hand, in order to avoid these ruptures, you can choose to live the discomfort of being comfortable in routine; it is comfortable, it is a comfort zone, you are fine where you are, but you are not living your dream. Living your dream also generates discomfort in and around you, but it makes you feel good because you are listening to the voice of the soul – your inner voice.

Be aware of your personal freedom. Individual history is not written and, in the case that it were, we don't know where the script is hidden. Perhaps it is hidden in your soul, which would explain the effect of déjà vu. Even so, you have to recreate it in each instant.

On the spiritual path, one speaks of the concept and lives the experience of rebirth. Each day you are born again, if you want to be, and each day you allow your ego, your limited self and your pride, to die. That way you allow the true being to emerge that is the being of light; the free being; the being that thinks about peace; that feels peace, that is peace and that has thoughts full of beauty and harmony.

In this daily rebirth you let go of the past, forgive, forget and bring out again your dream and your meaning for existence. If yesterday you made a mistake, you tripped, you fell, you were lazy, don't allow those things to continue today. You are reborn. This capacity to be reborn gives you great strength and vitality. You live without burdens.

In adolescence we have dreams and then, in the measure that we live through different situations and get older, it seems impossible to us that they might be fulfilled. We reconcile ourselves, accommodating ourselves to the reality that we find ourselves in, and things become routine and ordinary. That spark has been lost – that magic that there would be if we were reconnected with the dream. Our burdens are like weights that prevent us from advancing light of luggage. For this not to happen any more and to be able to live in wholeness, we have to learn to be reborn. You are no longer who you were yesterday. Don't allow the disappointment of yesterday put you out today. Renew yourself. You can.

Life is a game, an adventure and a great theatre play. Learn to play, enjoy the game, keep good humour and a smiling heart. On the adventure of life, be brave. Don't feel failures or disappointments as a curse. Don't judge others so much, since this makes you lose faith and trust, and instead of living life as an adventure, you live it as a threat from which you have to defend yourself. Going onto the defensive prevents you from living the magic of the dream and the instant.

Live like an actor in the play; each scene comes and goes; new actors appear and others disappear. Don't lose yourself in the roles of others. Play your part well, without repressing your creative capacity.

If you participate in the game, you live the adventure and form part of the great work; your life fills with magic and full, unique and extraordinary moments.

The Value of the Essential

When what we do and live is full of meaning, we feel whole. Our energy flows and we fill everything we touch with our essence. To live the essential is to live what gives meaning to each thought, word, action, relationship and project.

We feel the essential with force when we are facing an imminent death. My friend José was given three months to live, and in the last conversation that I held with him, some days before his death, I perceived that he was nearer the angels than human beings. José talked to me of everything that is essential and told me that it is not worth clinging onto anything or fighting to have things or achieve a position to get the recognition of others. He transmitted to me the light that he felt. "You only have to be yourself, without defences. Let your light shine. Be without fear. Labels are no use at all," he told me.

He also shared with me that he wanted to carry out a project that he had dreamt of carrying out for years, but never did. He kept on postponing it until it was now too late for him. He asked me for my support so that it could be realised.

In the face of imminent death, on the one hand, one lets go of what is useless and lives what is essential, and on the other, one feels the need for all the dreams one has had to become reality. Carrying out the dream becomes a priority.

The value of the essential is everything that refers to the self – to your person. The essential lies in the power of being: the power of thinking, deciding, feeling, doing, acting, being, and finally, the power of transcending.

When the conscience, decision and action are aligned, what is essential flows and is transmitted in each one of our acts. The essential is in our consciousness and, if our decisions and actions are based on it, we live with coherence and integrity, and we transmit the essential to others.

In the area of being, the essential lies in authenticity, integrity and transparency. It also includes inner freedom, peace, personal governance, love, self-esteem, integrity and harmony.

In each area of our life, maintaining the essential is not to forget or compromise those principles and values. If, for you, it is essential to maintain your inner peace and your harmony, you won't have thoughts or carry out actions that endanger this peace; thoughts that do not harmonise and, therefore, destroy or go against what is essential for you.

In the area of relationships, the essential is love, under-standing, communication, dialogue and wholeness.

It is important that you are clear about what is essential for you. To give you some ideas and suggestions that help you to see what is truly essential, I include the list of essential values that a group of participants in one of my seminars created:

The essential values in the area of being are:
- Authenticity.
- Coherence.
- Energy.
- Freedom.
- Goodness.
- Happiness.
- Harmony.
- Honesty.
- Independence.
- Integrity.
- Love.
- Peace.
- Personal governance.
- Security.

The essential values in the area of relationships are:

- Acceptance.
- Friendship.
- Generosity.
- Patience.
- Respect.
- Tolerance.
- Understanding.

These essential values make up part of our dream, our paradise – what we really want to live. Our soul enjoys, dances and feels whole on living them.

To live the essential, there are some important factors that have to be taken into account:

The Value of the Important

The 'important' includes all the necessary means in order for the essential to be lived:

- Talents.
- Inner and outer resources.
- Facilities.
- Technology.
- Systems.
- Language.
- Work.
- Money.
- Relationships.

In the area of the important, there are also values like enthusiasm, perseverance, determination and bravery; values that help us to maintain and live the essential.

When the important finds itself again with the day to day, with circumstances and unforeseen situations, some factors that enter into the area of the necessary have to be taken into account.

The Value of the Necessary

It is necessary for you to use your time in giving priority to what is truly important.

In the encounter with the day to day we should know how to find ourselves at ease in spaces and use resources in such a way that we do not postpone the important. Often we get distracted; situations appear that we have to solve and we put off what is a priority until, we eventually come to forget it. Unfortunately, our life fills with ordinary and useless matters that distance us from the essential.

For the important to help you to live your dream and your freedom, it is necessary to discipline oneself, work and study. For example, we have seen that language or talents are important because they help us to live the essential. Language you have to study and work at to express yourself better, to communicate yourself and learn to dialogue. Many of the problems in relationships lie in bad communication. We want to say something, our intention is good, but the other has understood something else and we haven't understood each other; there wasn't true communication and the harmony was lost.

We need discipline in order to improve and refine our talents. We need study and knowledge in order to know how to manage them and fulfil their potential, in such a way for them to take us to excellence.

The necessary also incorporates all of that we need in order to live together, deal with and overcome things. Time, space and resources imply limits that we should know how to manage and with which we should live. To do so, we need creativity, clarity and to know how to prioritise.

When we are not creative, we don't have clear objectives and don't know how to prioritise; we easily devote ourselves to things that distance us from the essential and that enter into the area of the unnecessary.

The Vulgar and the Unnecessary

It is important to set ourselves priorities that help us to do what is necessary in order to devote ourselves to the important and, thus, live the essential. When we haven't set priorities, we get distracted. We have useless conversations, dispersed thoughts, we carry out tasks that are not necessary and, finally, we distance ourselves from the essential. We waste time and misspend our energy and our resources.

The vulgar is all that which distracts us from the important; it traps us in the unnecessary and distances us from the principles and values of the self.

When you place thoughts, tasks, conversations and people in front of yourself that distance you from your being and your essence, and they lead you to live superficiality, the ordinary and that which doesn't have meaning, you are giving priority to the unnecessary and you distance yourself from the essential. In this area of the unnecessary are also included staying trapped in the past, dependences, the beliefs that limit us and fears of the future. All this I have already dealt with in the previous chapters.

When you place in front of yourself, and you concern yourself with, what, by nature, tends to distance you from your spirit, your purpose and your being, you are using your time and energy in something unnecessary and you disconnect from your principles and from your essence.

We have seen these four areas:
- The essential.
- The important.
- The necessary.
- The unnecessary.

What can really help you is for you to clarify what it is that, in these moments of your life, in your circumstances and in your present situation, distances you from your dream and from the essential, and what it is that helps you and brings you close to it.

As well as what I have already laid out, these are some of the values and factors to be taken into account:

The following bring you close to the essential:
- Acceptance.
- An open attitude and mentality.
- Asking yourself sincere questions.
- Communication.
- Detachments.
- Effort.
- Flow.
- Going slower, slowing down the rhythm.
- Healthy habits.
- Silence.
- Tolerance.
- Training and discipline.
- Trust.
- Understanding.

The following distance you from your purpose:
- Conditionings.
- Confrontation.
- Dependencies.
- Fears.
- Getting comfortable.
- Hurries.
- Intolerance.
- Lack of communication.
- Laziness.
- Selfishness.
- Submission.
- Unnecessary desires.
- Wrong judgement.
- Wanting to control.

You can be clearer about it if you specify these factors according to the areas of application in your life:

Essential Value and Freedom

	BRINGS ME CLOSER	DISTANCES ME
	Important	Unnecessary
Being	Reflection, silence. Walking alone on the beach. Writing.	I think: I can't. Belief: impossible. Emotion: attachment. Getting stuck in my past.
Family	Sharing spaces of dialogue and reflexion. Detachment.	Fear of being different Dependencies
Profession/Work	Clarifying priorities. Concentration. Training.	Rumours. Submission. Laziness, lack of motivation, apathy.
Friendships	Acceptance. Trust. Say what I think.	Wrong judgement. Hurries.
Area		

Transcend

Each soul is potentially divine. The goal is to manifest this divinity within by controlling nature: external and internal. Do this either by work, or worship or psychic control or philosophy – by one, or more, or all of these – and be free. This is the whole of religion. Doctrines, or dogmas, or rituals, or books, or temples, or forms, are but secondary details.
Swami Vivekananda: *Raja yoga.*

To centre yourself on the essential, on what helps you to be yourself and gives meaning to your existence, you need to be beyond the trivial and the unnecessary. That requires the capacity to transcend and let go. Distance yourself from the situations that don't benefit you, the people that don't bring you anything and the conversations that cause unhappiness and are a waste of time and energy. To achieve it, you need to centre yourself with determination.

You can transcend on different levels: from the small and the insignificant to transcending the ego and submerging yourself in communion with the Light, the Universal and the Divine. Transcend earthly passions in order to reach spiritual wholeness and liberation; nirvana; the state beyond sound; salvation.

We look for salvation in order to relieve ourselves of spiritual, mental, emotional or physical suffering. One of the deepest sufferings is generated by the lack of identity and lack of meaning. Salvation is sought to fill this existential void. We put up with unhappiness and suffering to a certain point, but a moment comes, when the pain goes beyond our limits, when we begin to actively look for paths that help us to understand, relieve or transcend.

There are different motives that motivate us to transcend: from suffering to the love of silence, of the divine and/or God. In a state of pure contemplation in which there are no self-limitations, our consciousness transcends to an unlimited state of unity, transparency, love, peace and freedom.

We all have the capacity to enter into this transcendent space where silence wraps itself around us; a sweet silence, in which we open ourselves to tenderness. We become aware of the immense power that we have within. Silence and quiet, liberation and love, tenderness and power are combined in a state in which we have transcended the consciousness of the limited self, the physical body and temporary identities.

To reach this state, it is not necessary to go anywhere. It is a matter of leaving behind the consciousness trapped by the day to day, action, hurries, sound and the body. It is not to be in the clouds, you are in a real and palpable dimension. On experiencing it, your vision is extended and you free yourself of mental boxes.

Is our purpose to live in the day to day reality and try to transcend it? Or is our purpose to bring transcendence to day to day reality?

We are transcendent beings, of conscious and spiritual energy. Therefore, we can live in transcendence, in universal awareness and be here present, but without boundaries and without limits in our heart or our mind. That way, we live having a vision of all the potential that humanity has, and that each one of us has as part of it. It is to have the vision of an eagle: wide, from above, but aware of everything that there is and everything that takes place below. From this awareness, we live our daily reality – everything that we have to do, such as eat, drink, earn money and spend money.

Alternatively, you can live reality from the limited vision of the 'mosquito'; the small vision of the specific situation, totally in it with your mind, with your emotions trapped here and missing the global vision. From here you try from time to time, if you do try, to connect with a reality that is transcendent.

It is much more exciting to live from transcendence and bring that energy here than be here and try to go to some transcendent place. To achieve it, we have to get out of the mental boxes that I have already spoken of in previous chapters.

To transcend does not mean to flee from reality or to live in a fantasy. To transcend, it is not necessary to go to a monastery or distance yourself from social life. For me transcendence means that link between who I am and what I do here. The awareness and vision in a transcendent state links all the actions that I carry out, everything that I say, what I think and gives a global meaning to my life.

What really links and unites everything is love. Love is transcendent, as are also peace and happiness. They are universal values that connect us to each other. You express love to a Chinese person, a Japanese person, an Australian or someone from a Nordic country and the energy of love transcends all limitations: cultural, age, gender, skin colour; all this and more, love transcends it. It is a transcendent value when you live it out of freedom, not when you live it out of limited identity, fear, dependences and attachments.

Let us learn to live in consciousness without limits, without blocking beliefs and without dependences; in sum, let us live in transcendence. In that space the heart is wide, love flows, the mind is calmed and the past does not weigh us down.

In transcendence you are no longer narcissistic, self-centred or selfish. A divine power attracts you and you have the courage to hand yourself over to it. This courage is motivated by authentic love. You become an instrument through which the melody of that great energy and great love flows and sounds. This is what you live and transmit to others.

From this state of awareness we act with accuracy, without pressure, with love, without getting entangled, with clarity and calm, with determination, without forcing. We are connected to the true identity of being and there is no addiction to action. The being shines in its freedom and authenticity and does not hide behind actions, but rather is present in actions, without its state depending on the result of the same.

The Bhagavad-Gita (3, 25) describes this state as one of a wise person: "As the ignorant perform their duties with attachment to results, the learned may similarly act, but without attachment, for the sake of leading people on the right path." (3, 19), "Therefore, without being attached to the fruits of activities, one should act as a matter of duty, for by working without attachment one attains the Supreme."

How do we get back that power that is necessary to achieve this state? In silence we learn to transcend and connect to the divine energy. It is the energy of light, eternal and pure. Making this connection is like connecting oneself to the main battery. When a battery discharges, it is connected to another more powerful source of energy in order to recharge. In meditation, we connect our inner battery, our being, to the divine energy, to pure energy.

True power is within. It is not a matter of filling oneself from the outside in but rather a question of recovering that energy, that inner strength, and aligning consciousness with decision, word and action. It is a question of aligning reason and intuition, mind and heart. How do you readjust the dispersed energies so that there is this inner power and this alignment of your energy? In meditating you harmonise with the centre of your being and, from there, the divine energy helps you to transcend. You live the present moment and, at the same time, you live in the eternity of time.

We have the capacity to live in various dimensions of time. For example, when you are here but your mind is thinking about tomorrow or yesterday: you are here but you are not here. Your body is here but your mind is somewhere else.

Within your being, you find that extemporal space that lies behind your busy mind. It is possible to go into this space when your hands and your mind are still. When you achieve this control over your mind and you keep it silent, you manage to stay free although your hands are in action. You have reached the state described in the Bhagavad-Gita as karma yoga. Your mind and your heart are conscious of being and are connected to the divine and transcendent, although your hands work and your body moves. You dance between being the observer who observes and the actor who acts. You don't get lost in the action on acting or in thoughts on observing. You act well, in peace, with precision, harmony and serenity. You are fully present. You do not get distracted by your thoughts or by the actions of others; you don't relive memories or the old habits of the past. You are here. YOU ARE you with all your being.

You enjoy the game and the adventure. No mountain or barrier stops you, no branch traps you and nothing limits you. You don't see your destiny as far away and your dream is a reality. You live what you want to live. This is your freedom. You live in freedom.

Meditations

Freeing Myself

I sit down comfortably and I begin to relax my body taking advantage of the paused rhythm of my breathing. I feel my calmed breathing.

I listen to the sounds of the space that surrounds me.

In this moment I decide to separate my attention from them.

The world follows its rhythm, its movement, but I do not need to involve myself in it.

I let go of the strings that pull on my mind, the strings that pull on my intellect.

I let go of the strings of my responsibilities,

I let go of the strings of my relationships,

I let go of the strings of the different roles that I play throughout the day.

This moment is only for me, to be in my own company.

I concentrate all my attention, all my energy, gently, without forcing, on a point at the centre of my forehead.

The energy concentrates itself. I have let go of the strings that tied me.

From that place I can experience true freedom.

I free myself of any limited awareness of myself.

I free myself of any label of myself.

I go beyond my limited roles, beyond this physical world.

I am a spiritual being; I am a point of light, a spark of spiritual energy; aware and loving.

I feel the true freedom of experiencing my authentic identity – genuine.

I don't have to prove anything; simply be what I am in a natural way.

A peaceful and living being.

From this state of being I prepare myself to enter into action. I listen again to the sounds of my surroundings, aware that I choose at each moment what it is that is going to influence me and how I am going to respond.

I am in my True Essence

I feel comfortable and attentive.

I am conscious of my thoughts and I direct my attention to my breathing.

I breathe gently and deeply. I begin to feel how my body and mind relax.

I let go of the things from outside. I feel free, like an observer, beyond everything that surrounds me: people, objects, sounds, worries... Everything slips from my mind. They pass and go like the clouds in the sky, until they fade away and everything remains completely clear.

I open a door. It is the door of my inner world. I discover that it is like an immense ocean. In the depths of my being there is silence, peace, calm and serenity. I go within.

I let go of the past and I see it disappear.

I submerge myself in this unlimited ocean, where all the mundane, negative thoughts melt away.

Before me, there opens a path of light that takes me to the depths where my true essence is found.

I see a star, marvellous and radiant with light.

From it emanate rays of peace and love, towards me.

My mind is tranquilised; it becomes silent and peaceful.

My thoughts are full of light, of peace, of love. I feel a profound acceptance and serenity inside me. In this space of silence I am with myself.

I feel free, light, peaceful and free of worries. I am at peace. I feel peace. I am free. I am myself.

Now it is time to return. I breathe gently and I am aware of the place I am in. I feel tranquillity, silence, peace, wellbeing.

My eyes and my face express this wellbeing.

I feel myself free.

I feel well with myself and with others.

Freeing Myself of My Dark Zones

Breathe deeply. Relax, calm yourself, while you let go of the air slowly. Become serene and feel a sensation of peace and wellbeing. Maintain this serenity in breathing in. Free yourself of tensions on letting go of the air.

I sit down comfortably, like an observer in silence. I stop paying attention to everything around me: objects, people, responsibilities, places.

I centre my mind on the present moment.

The serenity, the tranquillity, wrap around me.

In this calm I can see the dark corners of my being. They are like shadows.

I see the fears, the anxieties, the guilt, the bitterness, the selfishness, the unhappiness.

They are weaknesses that lie in some corner of me.

I accept that there are these dark areas within me. I observe them and I realise that I am not that darkness, I am not that weakness; it is not real; it is like a shadow.

I focus now on what is real; all my energy concentrates itself in the centre of my forehead and I visualise the energy centred like a point of light.

It is a star of love, of peace, of wellbeing.

I only have to access these original qualities and allow these energies to strengthen my soul. To do so, I continue to observe with calm, with patience. I don't allow my mind to judge or analyse what is happening to me. Everything that has happened to me forms part of the past.

I have learned from my mistakes. I forgive myself. I forgive others.

I observe feeling who I am. I am a being of light; a peaceful being that irradiates light, like a small candle that lights up a dark room and dissipates the darkness that there is in my inner room.

Aware of whom I am; I open myself to receive the presence of a benevolent Being of Light that emanates infinite love, peace and happiness.

It is an ocean of love that can dissolve all my fears and melt the pain and suffering that there is within the soul.

I open my heart and I go towards this ocean, saying to it "Here are my fears, here are my dark areas. They are Yours. They are no longer useful to me. I hand them over to You. I absorb your love and allow it to reach each dark corner of my being. I feel how your love touches my fears, they dissolve and I am freed."

The weaknesses no longer have power over me.

God is with me. He accepts me as I am, he comforts me, there is nothing to fear and I feel secure; in an immense peace, in the light of being.

I maintain the divine presence in my being; a presence that dissipates the darkness and brings out the clarity of beauty.

I Reconnect with the Meaning of My Life

I sit in a comfortable position.
I relax my body.
I breathe deeply and let go of tensions.
I centre myself in the present moment.
I concentrate my mind.
Whatever happens around me, I keep myself centred.
I disconnect from external situations.
I enter into the space of inner silence.
The thoughts diminish and my mind relaxes fully.
I connect to the essence of my being.
I am love.
I love each part of my body. I relax it.
I love each thought that I create, it is my creation.
I generate gentle thoughts, tender, relaxing.
I feel the energy of love that emerges from within me.

I give off love towards what surrounds me.

I give off love towards people.

I give off love towards nature and the planet.

I am love.

I channel this love towards everything I think, feel, do and transmit.

I reconnect thus with the meaning of my life;

to give and share the best of me;

to open myself without fears;

sharing my strengths, my virtues, my qualities.

I transmit and share that vibration of beauty, love and serenity.

I give off peace.

I decide to give off the best of my being.

And thus I prepare myself to go on.

I Am Who I Want to be in the Game of Life

I relax my body.

I breathe deeply and let go of tensions.

I centre myself on this present moment.

On the screen of my mind, I visualise who I want to be;

if I were not afraid, who I would be.

I visualise myself without fears.

I let go of all labels, all roles that I play.

Now I AM.

I am free.

I am peace.

I am shining.

I am totally free, beyond all limitations.

I enter into the dimension without frontiers.

I stop thinking so much; I simply feel the presence of my being.

I am who I want to be.

I am me.

I do not need to justify myself.

I do not need to give explanations.

I enter into the sacred space of being.

I connect to my inner beauty.

I irradiate the energy of the beauty that there is in me.

I let go of the branches.

I fly.

I fly high.

Beyond the body, above this place, the people that surround me,

Beyond the houses and the streets, beyond the clouds, I fly towards the dimension of light where no physical limitation ties me down.

I feel the breeze and the wind that caress my being.

I let myself be taken by the sensation of freedom that the flight gives me.

I see the planet Earth from above.

I recognise that everything there below is a game.

I relax: everything is a game.

I am a player in the game of life.

Everything is relative.

I simply have to learn to play the game being who I am.

Now, it is time to return. I am here, present.

My breathing calmed.

My soul relieved.

Now I know that, whenever I want, I can fly,

Being an observer of the game,

And live it with joy and serenity.

Being My Best Friend

Relax your body and allow yourself to be fully present, here, listening to the sounds around you, feeling what you feel.

Now send love to each part of your body: your feet, your legs, your back, your shoulders, your face and your eyes. Send love to each part of your body until you feel it from head to toe.

Visualise how your energy concentrates itself at the inner part of the centre of your forehead.

Observe the screen of your mind, and try to make each thought that you generate full of the energy of love that invades you slowly.

The energy of love is present in each thought that appears in your mind.

I love who I am.

I let go of who I am not.

I let go of what I don't like of myself.

I visualise a trunk next to me and I put into it all that I don't like of myself.

I let go of it, throwing it into the trunk.

I free myself of everything that I do not like of myself.

I visualise that I am at the beach. I take the trunk and I throw it into the sea.

Throwing the trunk, I let go of all that I don't like of myself.

I give up my dark areas. I help myself valuing who I am.

The presence of my true being emerges; a strong, energetic presence; serene and full of vitality.

I am life.

I encourage myself.

I can achieve it.

I can let go and be free.

I love myself.

I am life energy.

I let this energy flow.

I get back the vitality of being.

As you spend time with yourself in this way, you will see how your insecurity begins to disappear and new possibilities appear before you.

Appreciating the Best of Myself

Sit down in silence, relax, breathe deeply and create a space within you.

Go within and feel yourself looking at your being in a different way.

Look what beautiful things you have inside you and learn to recognise them.

You have so much to offer, so much to give…

Keep a positive attitude and concentrate on that which makes you happy.

I create a beautiful image of myself where I see myself as free.

Free of negative feelings, with a clean heart and a mind at peace.

I can feel and see the greatness of my soul, discover that I am special and unique;

strong and brave. I come back to being my own friend.

I love myself, I accept myself and I respect myself. I am honest and sincere with my own feelings.

I say what I think with love.

I appreciate and value the qualities and virtues of others.

I feel fine being myself, in that space, in that room that there is within me, where I am secure and safe, where I can enjoy the marvellous thing that is my own company.

Here I find the creativity, the love, the calm and the silent peace that there is in the deepest part of me.

I am awake and full of life. I am happy.

I am at peace.

I feel peace. I share peace.

I feel free.

I love and respect myself.

I prepare myself to enter into action, maintaining my self-esteem.

I Live My Dream

I relax. I let go of tensions.

I reduce my speed of thought.

I relax my thinking.

An energy of calm and wellbeing invades my being and leaves me well.

I am fine.

I let go of what doesn't let me be well.

Now, I let it go.

What is it that my soul truly longs for?

What do I want in my life?

I listen to the answer that arises from the inside of the self.

I let the answer come out spontaneously.

I don't worry about it.

I visualise what I want and where I want to reach.

Now I fly; I fly towards the destiny that I dream of.

I visualise myself being what I want to be.

Without fears, without strings that tie me.

I am who I want to be.

I see myself like that, having achieved it.

I enjoy some moments of this experience.

I can achieve my dream.

I have to visualise it as if I had already achieved it.

This strengthens my capacity to achieve it.

I can achieve it.

Now I return to the present moment.

I prepare myself to enter into action with this conviction.

I will make my dream reality.

I Can

I relax my body into a comfortable posture.

I let go of tensions.

I concentrate my mind.

I am the owner of my mind.

I direct my thoughts.

I can.

I can calm my mind.

I enter into silence.

I say to my mind, "Don't think, let the stories and circumstances carry on outside of here, let them follow their course. The earth turns, everything moves, but now, oh mind, stop thinking,"

Simply feel the peace.

The presence of being, that embraces the mind in a relaxing embrace.

I can think less.

I can stop thinking now.

I feel the silence.

I can create the thoughts that I want.

I can be me.

I can feel peace.

I can feel freedom; letting go; being.

In the presence of being here and now

I have all the power in my hands.

I concentrate my energy.

I can create my destiny.

I am the ruler of my mind.

I am the ruler of my life.

My Inner Wealth

I go into the silence.

I go to the encounter with my own being.

I leave behind everything that distances me from my own awareness.

I free myself from the ties of the past.

I overcome the limitations created by my mind.

I open my consciousness towards the vision of the spiritual being that is me.

I submerge myself in the depths of my own awareness.

I go on to the places where silence and peace reigns.

This is my kingdom; a world of calm, of serenity.

I connect with the eternal energies of peace, love and happiness.

I feel that my heart opens like a flower

And gives off its fragrance of peace, of love and of happiness.

I enjoy all the wealth of my inner world.

The light of the soul shines within me with all its splendour.

I feel how its glow lightens my being.

I share with the world the light of my consciousness.

I am like a lighthouse for the world.

I feel the happiness of experiencing my own nature.

I am a luminous and light being.

I can go beyond any physical limitation; I can fly.

I unfold the wings of happiness, enthusiasm and joy.

I fly freely and I feel capable of reaching my highest goals.

I am a unique and special being.

The sun of happiness shines in my heart.

Bibliography

Bhaktivedanta Swami Prabhupāda, A.C.: Bhagavad-gita As It Is. (The Bhaktivedanta Book Trust, USA., 1983)

Church, Anthea: Angels. (Brahma Kumaris Information Services. London, UK, 1997)

Dyer, Dr. Wayne W.: Your Erroneous Zones. (Avon Books, New York, USA, 2001)

Fromm, Erich: The Fear of Freedom. (Routledge, London, 2001)

Fromm, Erich: Escape from Freedom. (Henry Holt, New York, USA)

George, Mike: Discover Inner Peace. (Duncan Baird Publishers. London, UK, 1999)

George, Mike: Don't get Mad get Wise. (O Books, UK 2007) (New York, USA)

George, Mike: The 7 AHA!s of Highly Enlightened Souls (John Hunt Publishers, UK 2005)

George, Mike: In the Light of Meditation. (O Books, UK, 2004) (New York, USA)

Krishnamurti: The First and Last Freedom. (HarperCollins Publishers, New York, USA, 1975)

Krishnamurti: A Flame of Learning, Krishnamurti with teachers. (Mirananda, The Netherlands, 1993)

Krishnamurti: On Freedom. (HarperCollins Publishers, New York, USA, 2003)
British edition: On Freedom. (Gollancz, London, 2006)

De Mello, Anthony: The Way to Love. (Image Book, Doubleday, New York, USA, 1995)

Melloni Ribas, Javier (2003): El Uno en lo múltiple. Aproximación a la diversidad y unidad de las religiones. Editorial Sal Terrae. Santander, Spain

O'Donnell, Ken: La última frontera. (Asociación Brahma Kumaris, Barcelona, 2006)

Osho: Satyam, Shivam, Sundaram: Truth, Godliness and Beauty. (Osho International Foundation, 1987)

Pemell, Judith: The Soul Illuminated. (Lothian Books, Melbourne, Australia, 2003)

Pinkerton, Margaret: Moving on. (Eternity Ink, Sydney, Australia, 1996)

Robbins, Anthony: Awaken the Giant Within. (Simon & Schuster Inc., New York, USA, 1991)

Robbins, Anthony: Unlimited Power. (Simon & Schuster Inc., New York, USA, 1986)

Sanllorente, Jaume (2007): Sonrisas de Bombay. El viaje que cambió mi destino. Plataforma Editorial. Barcelona.

Strano, Anthony: Eastern Thought for the Western Mind. (BK Publications, London, 2006)

Subirana Vilanova, Miriam and Ribalta, Ramón: Who Rules in Your Life. (O Books, Winchester. UK, 2008) (Nueva York, EE UU)

Subirana Vilanova, Miriam: Dare to Live. (O Books, Winchester, UK, 2008) (Nueva York, EE UU)

Swami Vivekananda: Raja yoga. (RamaKrishna-Vivekananda Center, New York, USA, 1982)

Torralba, Francesc (2008): El sentit de la vida. Ara Llibres. Badalona. Barcelona, Spain.

Raja Yoga Meditation Centres of the Brahma Kumaris World Spiritual University

The more than 9000 meditation centres of the Brahma Kumaris Organisation in 100 countries offer courses in positive thinking, overcoming stress, self-esteem, Raja Yoga meditation and personal leadership.
The Brahma Kumaris World Spiritual University is an international organisation, which works in all areas of society for a positive change. Created in 1937, at present it offers, and actively participates in, a wide range of educational programmes for the development of human and spiritual values.

For more information visit the web page:
www.bkwsu.org

About the Author

Doctor in Fine Arts, University of Barcelona.

Miriam Subirana shares her profession as a painter and writer with being a coach, a lecturer and a teacher of meditation and positive thinking. She coordinates programmes, projects, seminars and retreats, the object of which are to re-find and live one's identity and enjoy a fuller life.

She gives lectures and seminars in different centres and cities of Spain, Europe, America, Asia and Australia.

She has shown her work in galleries and exhibition halls in Spain, Portugal, France, Denmark, England, New York, Sao Paolo, Hong Kong, Mexico and Kuwait, amongst others.

She has directed the creation of two galleries of spiritual art in Mount Abu and Agra (India).

She is the creator and director of the space YESOUISI, international centre of Art and Spirituality: www.yesouisi.es

Her two books, *Quién manda en tu vida. Reflexiones sobre la soberanía personal* and *Atreverse a vivir. Reflexiones sobre el miedo, la valentía y la plenitud*, have been re-edited various times and have been published in English with the titles, *Who rules in your life. Reflections on personal power* and *Dare to Live. Reflections on Fear, Courage and Wholeness* (O Books, 2008). She also publishes articles on themes of personal growth. She has recorded numerous CDs with guided meditations.

www.miriamsubirana.com
mira@miriamsubirana.com

BOOKS

O is a symbol of the world, of oneness and unity. In different cultures it also means the "eye," symbolizing knowledge and insight. We aim to publish books that are accessible, constructive and that challenge accepted opinion, both that of academia and the "moral majority."

Our books are available in all good English language bookstores worldwide. If you don't see the book on the shelves ask the bookstore to order it for you, quoting the ISBN number and title. Alternatively you can order online (all major online retail sites carry our titles) or contact the distributor in the relevant country, listed on the copyright page.

See our website **www.o-books.net** for a full list of over 500 titles, growing by 100 a year.

And tune in to myspiritradio.com for our book review radio show, hosted by June-Elleni Laine, where you can listen to the authors discussing their books.

MySpiritRadio